DISCOVERING CANADA

Black Heritage

ROBERT LIVESEY & A.G. SMITH

Published in Canada by Fitzhenry & Whiteside, 195 Allstate Parkway, Markham, Ontario L3R 4T8

Published in the United States by Fitzhenry & Whiteside, 311 Washington Street, Brighton, Massachusetts 02135

www.fitzhenry.ca   godwit@fitzhenry.ca

10   9   8   7   6   5   4   3   2

Library and Archives Canada Cataloguing in Publication
Livesey, Robert, 1940-
        Black heritage / Robert Livesey ; illustrated by A.G. Smith.
(Discovering Canada)
Includes index.
ISBN 1-55005-137-7
        1. Blacks-Canada-History-Juvenile literature.
        I. Smith, A. G. (Albert Gray), 1945-   II. Title.   III. Series.

FC106.B6L58   2006   j971'.00496   C2005-907670-4

Fitzhenry & Whiteside acknowledges with thanks the Canada Council for the Arts, and the Ontario Arts Council for their support of our publishing program. We acknowledge the financial support of the Government of Canada through the Book Publishing Industry Development Program (BPIDP) for our publishing activities.

Canada Council
for the Arts
Conseil des Arts
du Canada

ONTARIO ARTS COUNCIL
CONSEIL DES ARTS DE L'ONTARIO

Cover and interior design by Daniel Crack, Kinetics Design

Printed in Canada

Dedicated to all Black Canadians, past, present, and future who have, or will, contribute their best to Canada.

A special thanks to Fred Gray; Robert Coté; Fred Hayward, U.E.; Josie Hazen; Linda Biesenthal; Sheryn Posen and Nhi Vo, Canada's Sports Hall of Fame; Brian and Shanon Prince, Buxton Museum; Scott McLeish, Statistics Canada; Gillian Small, Ontario Black History Society; Adrienne Shadd, descendant of Mary Ann Shadd; Howard Aster, publisher, Mosaic Press, for the book, A Fly In A Pail Of Milk, *by Herb Carnegie; "Theology3," a.k.a. Theo Steryannis, Program Director at 4Unity Productions; Peter Meyler, co-author with his brother David of* A Stolen Life: Searching for Richard Pierpoint; *Peter McCarney, publisher, McCarney & Associates; the librarians at the Oakville Public Library and the University of Windsor Library.*

Contents

Introduction

Today, Black Canadians live in every province and territory of Canada and contribute to all aspects of our society, but that was not always true. In early Canada, Black people were often threatened with prejudice and violence. Their history was a difficult struggle that required strength, determination, and bravery. Many refused to be intimidated and risked, or sometimes lost, their lives trying to survive.

Imagine what it would be like if people kidnapped you from your warm and sunny homeland and then shipped you for more than six weeks in the cold, dark hold of a slave ship across a rough and cruel ocean to a strange land where your new masters spoke unfamiliar languages. You would never see your family or friends again. Your arms and legs would be chained in irons and you would be packed tightly with hundreds of other unfortunate captives, with very little food or water. One-third of your fellow prisoners would die during the harsh trip, which would become known as the "Middle Passage." When you reached the destination, you would be sold on an auction block, like an animal, to an unknown master who could force you to work long hours at hard labour, with the threat of torture or death if you objected.

It is estimated that 55 to 80 million Africans were torn from their families, culture, and religion and forced into slavery. Many were sold in South and North America or the Caribbean Islands to work on plantations. Some ended up in Canada.

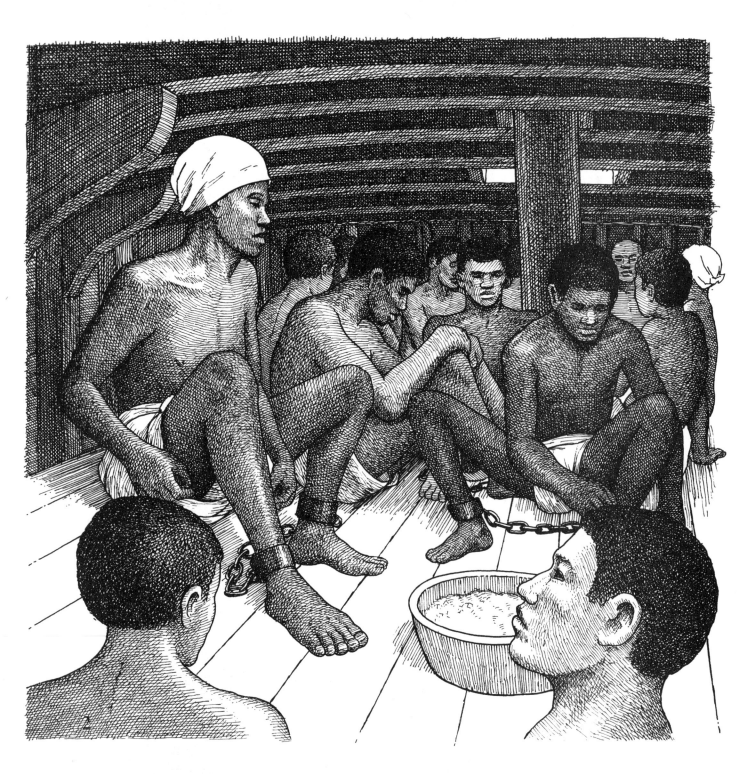

CHAPTER 1 *Slaves*

Mattieu da Costa, Olivier Le Jeune, and Others

A slave is a person who is captured and forced to work without pay. Slaves are treated as property rather than as human beings. Slavery has existed all over the world since early times; it still exists in some countries today. Ancient Greeks and Romans had slaves, and before Europeans arrived in North America, some Native peoples made slaves of their enemies.

The African Slave Trade

In the early 1600s, Portuguese and Spanish merchants began to import African slaves across the Atlantic Ocean to their colonies in South and Central America because they needed inexpensive labourers to develop the new lands. Between 1562 and 1567, several shiploads of Black slaves were brought from Africa and sold in the Spanish settlements by an English pirate, Captain John Hawkins. In 1619, African slaves were sold in Jamestown, Virginia, in British North America, by a Dutch sea captain.

From the beginning of the colonies in the New World, there was a great need for cheap labour. Most attempts to use the Native peoples were not successful, and importing poor servants or white prisoners from Europe also failed. Large numbers of workers were needed. By the 1620s, slavery was sanctioned. Africans were kidnapped from their homes and shipped across the Atlantic Ocean. Slave trading became a profitable business.

Slave traders raided the villages of unsuspecting Africans, capturing mainly older children, teenagers, and young adults in their twenties or thirties.

3

Slaves had to be strong and healthy to survive the deadly ocean voyage and the hard labour awaiting them. Ruthless African chiefs sold their own people to the slave traders in exchange for guns, tobacco, or alcohol.

Most slaves were shipped from two areas of Africa: the "Slave Coast" and the Portuguese colony of Angola. The victims spoke over 800 different African languages. By the mid 1600s, 10,000 slaves a year were being sent across the ocean; by the 1700s, it was 60,000 per year. By 1760, there were about 400,000 slaves in the colonies. Most were forced to pick cotton on the large plantations in the southern colonies of Maryland, Virginia, Georgia, and the Carolinas. Gangs of Black workers were guarded by slave drivers who worked them without mercy from sunrise to sunset.

In Canada, the farms were smaller, and the cold climate limited the growing season. Most Blacks in Canada became household servants or sometimes freemen working for a living. By the time slavery was finally abolished by Great Britain in 1834, most Blacks living in Canada had already been granted their freedom.

Blacks in New France

Over a period of 125 years, there were about 4,000 slaves in New France. Most were young and died on average at 17 or 18 years of age.

The first known Black resident of Canada was Mattieu (or Matthew) da Costa. In 1605, he was an employee of Pierre de Gua, sieur de Monts, the governor of the settlement of Port Royal in New France. He lived in the famous *habitation* established by Samuel de Champlain and was a member of L'Ordre de Bon Temps (The Order of Good Cheer). Because he was very good at learning new languages, Mattieu acted as Champlain's interpreter with the Mi'kmaq people. He had once been a slave of the Portuguese, but he was regarded as an equal and free man in the colony.

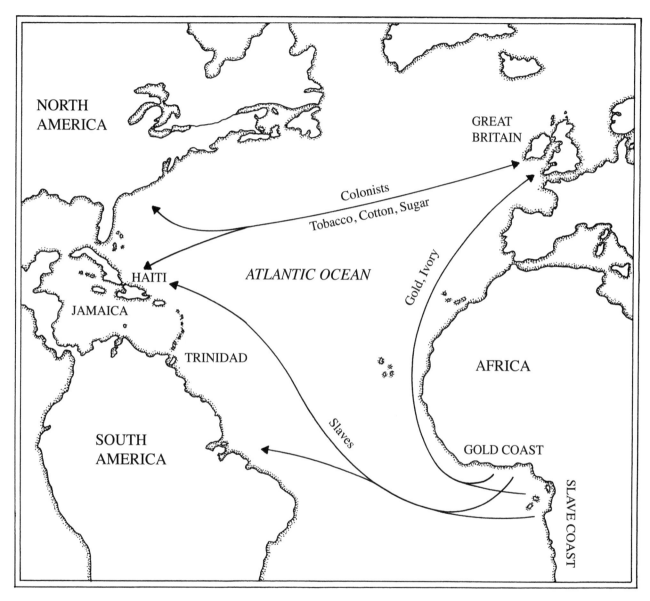

NORTH
AMERICA

GREAT
BRITAIN

Colonists
Tobacco, Cotton, Sugar

Gold, Ivory

ATLANTIC OCEAN

HAITI

JAMAICA

AFRICA

TRINIDAD

Slaves

SOUTH
AMERICA

GOLD COAST

SLAVE COAST

The Slave Trade

In 1628, the first known Black slave arrived in Canada with an English privateer, Captain David Kirke, who captured the Quebec fortress from Champlain. The boy was sold to a French clerk in Quebec. In 1632, the English returned the fortress to the French. Olivier Le Cardif rescued the youth. He was taught Christianity by Father Le Jeune and baptized Olivier Le Jeune, a combination of the names of his rescuer and his priest. Olivier was set free in 1638 and worked as a servant until he died in 1654.

In 1734, a 25-year-old Black woman, Marie-Joseph Angélique, learned that, after the death of her master, she was to be resold. She set fire to her owner's home as a distraction during an attempt to escape. The fire spread quickly and destroyed 46 houses in the settlement of Montreal. She was captured, tortured, hanged, and her corpse burned.

6

When the British conquered New France in 1759, it became part of British North America. At that time, there were more than 1,000 Black slaves around Montreal and the French fort of Louisbourg.

Blacks in the Maritimes

When the Maritimes was part of New France, there were records of Blacks living in the area. Mattieu da Costa was at Port Royal when it was founded in 1605. In 1686, a Black man known as La Liberté lived on Cape Sable Island. The French governor of Louisbourg in 1739 owned a slave from the island of Martinique. After the British took control from the French, the English lieutenant-governor of Nova Scotia reported in 1767 that the population of 13,374 included 104 Blacks. About half of them lived in Halifax.

Slaves and Free Blacks in English Canada

In 1760, after the Seven Years' War, slavery became legal in British North America, and slaves were brought to the Maritimes. Slavery was not popular in the area after 1800, but it was not officially abolished until 1834.

After the American Revolution started in 1783, many British Loyalists immigrated to Canada. This brought two groups of Blacks to the frontier settlements of Canada. Between 2,000 and 3,000 Black slaves came with their white Loyalist masters to Nova Scotia, Lower Canada, and Upper Canada.* Loyalist-owned slaves also lived on Prince Edward Island, Cape Breton, and Newfoundland. The second group of Blacks to immigrate to Canada in large numbers were free Black Loyalists, who had fought for the British against the American rebels.

* Today, Lower Canada is the province of Quebec, and Upper Canada
  is the province of Ontario.

Slave Saying

Slaves had no rights. They were expected to obey, not to think for themselves. They were kept obedient by the fear of physical abuse and the lack of formal education. One popular slave saying around 1830 was "Got one mind for the white folk to see, 'nother for what I know is me."

Panis

By 1759, when the British defeated the French and New France became part of British North America, there were reported to be 3,604 slaves in New France, but only 1,132 were Black slaves. The majority were Pawnees, known as *panis*, who were kidnapped from their homes in the present-day state of Nebraska and forced into slavery.

Loyal Lover

Marie-Joseph Angélique, the slave who set the early settlement of Montreal on fire in her attempt to escape, had fallen in love with a white man named Claude Thibault, who encouraged her to escape with him to New England. Although she was tortured four times to force her to confess to starting the blaze, she never revealed her accomplice. Throughout her suffering, Marie-Joseph remained loyal to her lover.

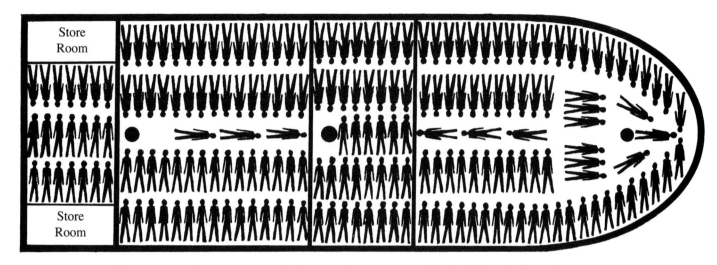

This image of an overcrowded slave ship was used by British abolitionist societies.

Marrying Slaves

In New France, owners sometimes married their slaves. The marriages were performed by the church, and the slaves became free citizens. Thirty-four marriages to *panis* slaves and eleven marriages to Black slaves were recorded in the early settlement. The *panis* marriages were mainly French men marrying Native women. The Black marriages were mainly French women marrying their Black slaves. About 103 children were born from these unions, and those children married and had many descendants.

Make an African Drum

Drums have always been a very important part of African culture. When slaves were brought to the southern U.S., the Christian slave owners prohibited the making and playing of drums and dancing. They believed that drums were pagan and sinful!

What you need:
- two flower pots, 15-20 cm in diameter
- glue or a nut, bolt, and two washers
- two pieces of thin leather or rubber (inner tube),
    5 cm larger in diameter than the pots
- heavy string or cord

What to do:
1. Attach the bottoms of the two pots with glue or a nut, bolt, and washers.
2. Decorate the pots.
3. From the rubber or leather pieces, cut two circles that are 5 cm larger in diameter than the tops of the pots.
4. Punch the same number of holes in each piece.
5. String the vertical cord between the two drum heads as shown on the next page. If you use leather, soak it in water first.
6. String the tightening cord around the vertical cords, looping around each vertical cord where they cross. Tighten the cord to adjust the tone, and tie the cord off. Have fun playing your drum.

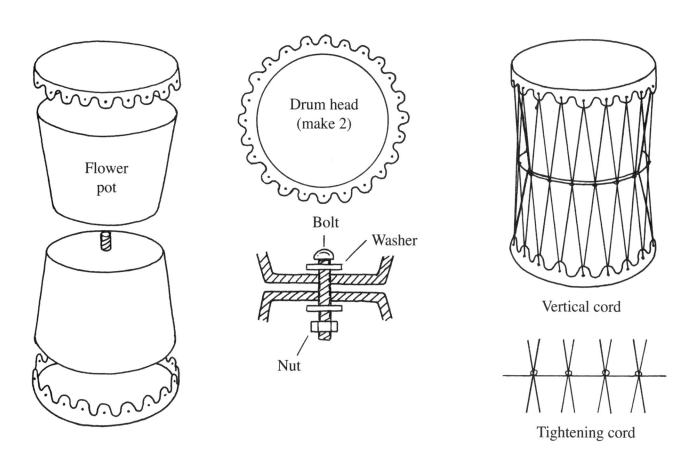

Flower pot

Drum head (make 2)

Bolt

Washer

Nut

Vertical cord

Tightening cord

AFRICAN DESIGN

Loyalists

Rose Fortune, Thomas Peters, and Others

Black communities developed in Canada more than 200 years ago.

When the rebels won the American Revolution, the British were forced to withdraw from the colonies. They offered land grants in Canada to all the Loyalists who had fought with them. About 40,000 British Loyalists migrated to start fresh lives in the Canadian wilderness.

There were only about 100 free Black settlers in Nova Scotia before over 3,500 free Black Loyalists arrived between 1782 and 1784. In addition, thousands of Black slaves came with their white Loyalist masters. White and Black Loyalists also settled in Upper and Lower Canada.

George Washington, the first American president, and the American Revolution are symbols of freedom and independence, but at the time, the new democratic rights did not include Blacks, women, or poor white people who did not own land. Washington owned hundreds of slaves who laboured on his prosperous Mount Vernon plantation. Democracy for all American citizens would come much later.

Many American Blacks did gain freedom as a result of the war, but it was offered by the British, not the Americans. In 1775, Lord Dunmore, governor of Virginia, offered freedom to the slaves of rebels, if they agreed to fight with the British. About 300 former slaves formed a regiment under the governor's name. They wore the slogan "Liberty to Slaves" across their chests.

The British later made the same offer to the slaves of rebels throughout the colonies. At the time, one-sixth of the population in all the colonies was Black. After the revolution, the British continued to offer freedom to the rebels' slaves, but not to the slaves of British Loyalists in Canada. Some American colonies responded with harsh new laws that allowed slave owners to sell or kill any fugitive slaves who were attempting to escape.

During the summer and fall of 1783, a fleet of 183 ships began to make trips from New York City to Nova Scotia and to what was soon to become New Brunswick, carrying about 35,000 Loyalists to safety. The ships travelled in fleets of a dozen or more vessels for protection from the vicious American privateers who were waiting to rob and kill the refugees. Other Loyalists travelled overland to Upper and Lower Canada.

The Company of Negroes was one of the first groups of Loyalists to arrive in Nova Scotia from Boston in 1776. In 1783, many thousands of other Black Loyalists came to Nova Scotia.

Land Grants

The Loyalists were promised free land grants, but the line-ups and waiting periods were long. The officials assigning the land grants to the new arrivals were overwhelmed by the numbers and demands of the frustrated new settlers, who were anxious to start building their homes.

The rules for issuing land grants did not favour Blacks or poor whites. People who suffered the greatest loss of property in the war were served first. They tended to be the wealthy whites who had owned large estates. Poorer refugees were supposed to be given 40 hectares for the head of the family and 20 additional hectares for each family member, including wives, children, and slaves. The size of the lots given to soldiers was based on their rank in the army. For example, an officer would receive 400 hectares, but an ordinary soldier would get only 40. Because the Blacks had been poorer citizens, former slaves, and rarely officers in the army, they often were served last and given the smallest amount of land.

Birchtown

As Blacks created their own communities in Nova Scotia, others began to arrive. By 1784, the Black community of Birchtown near Shelburne (originally Port Roseway) had grown to 2,700 people, the largest community of Blacks in Nova Scotia. The Black Pioneers, an all-Black regiment of Loyalists, helped to build Birchtown.

Stephen Blucke

Stephen Blucke, born in Barbados to a Black mother and a white father, had commanded a fighting unit in New Jersey. He became the leader of the Black community and the largest landowner in Birchtown. His land grant was 500 hectares. His wife, Margaret, had bought her own freedom in New York at age 14, and later the freedom of a girl, Isabella Gibbons. When they arrived in 1783, Stephen was 31, Margaret was 40, and Isabella was 20.

Blucke had received his land grant by 1786, but only 184 of 649 Black applicants in Birchtown had obtained their grants by 1787. Many waited for four years, and some were left out entirely. Because he could read and write, Blucke became a powerful authority. He frequently aided fellow Blacks who were presenting petitions for land or supplies. He organized crews to build roads, and he became a teacher of the Black students. Blucke's fishing boat was one of the first to be built by Blacks in Shelburne.

Unfortunately, Blucke's life ended in disgrace and mystery. He became involved with Isabella, and they had a daughter, Frances. His wife moved back to New York in shame. He was accused of taking money that others had trusted him to hold. Then, he suddenly disappeared. His torn clothes were discovered on Pell Road. Some thought he was attacked by wild animals, but his body was never found.

Digby

Black Loyalists also settled in and around Digby, Nova Scotia, creating the second largest Black community in the province. Thomas Peters, a fugitive slave from North Carolina, joined the Black Pioneers in 1776 to fight against the rebels. He and Murphy Still had been sergeants in the army, and for six long years starting in 1783, they wrote to the authorities on behalf of the soldiers, complaining about the delays in issuing the promised land grants. Only 76 small lots had been granted in the town by 1789. In total, about 500 Black Loyalists obtained land grants in Nova Scotia.

Little Tracadie

Thomas Brownspriggs, the head of the Black community of Little Tracadie, was well educated and well respected by both whites and Blacks. Governor Parr appointed him as the agent to create a Black settlement. He obtained grants of 16 hectares for all 74 of his Black settlers in 1787, the same day he presented the petition for land. Brownspriggs was a teacher and a leader in the Anglican Church.

Preston

A community of 29 Black families settled at Preston, close to Dartmouth, in 1783. Yet one year later only 10 had received land grants. The problem was not the lack of land, but the cost of surveying the lots. Most Blacks could not afford to pay a surveyor.

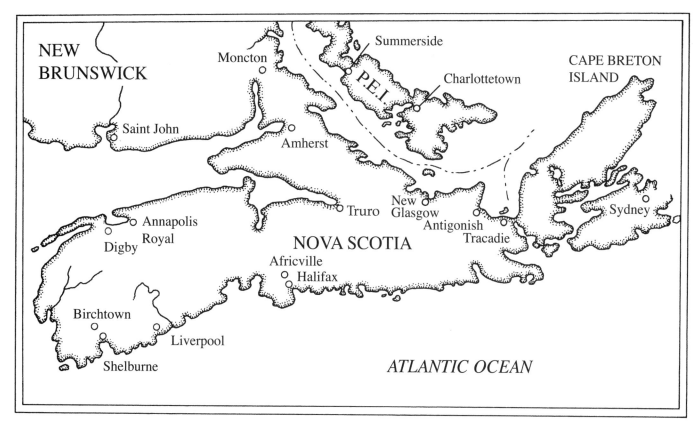

Black Settlements in the Maritimes

New Brunswick Black Settlements

When the province of New Brunswick was created in 1784, it had a total Black population of 874, which included 441 slaves and 433 newly arrived free Blacks. All 433 free Blacks were given small town lots in Saint John, and some got together to form companies (there were three such companies in total) that were given 121 additional farming lots of 20 hectares. Most of the Blacks were employed in the town, rather than in farming the land. The first successful all-Black settlement was at Otnabog in 1812.

17

Prince Edward Island

Before 1799, Prince Edward Island was called St. John's Island, and as early as 1784, there were 42 Black servants and slaves living there.

Church Leaders

Many Blacks had to adjust not only to the cold climate and rugged frontier life, but to the idea of being free, since they had been slaves before they arrived. They relied on their churches, schools, and families for support in their new settlements.

Evangelistic preachers, such as Joseph Leonard, Cato Perkins, Boston King, and Moses Wilkinson, emerged to lead the people. Moses was both blind and lame. David George, a former slave, had started the Silver Bluff Baptist Church in South Carolina, the first Black congregation in North America. In Nova Scotia, he continued his preaching as a Black Loyalist. Hector Peters was an evangelist in Nova Scotia and later the first Baptist missionary in Sierra Leone in Africa.

White Race Riots

Many of the Black Loyalists of Nova Scotia became sharecroppers, hired labourers, or servants, but the poor economy led to rivalry with poor whites who resented the Blacks taking jobs that they needed. The conflict turned to hatred and prejudice that caused a race riot in July 1784 in Shelburne and Birchtown. It lasted for 10 days, forcing Governor Parr to send the army and navy to restore order.

Exodus to Africa

Like the white Loyalists, Black Loyalists were supposed to receive free land and financial aid from the British government to resettle in Canada, but many did not. The line-ups were long, the rules were often confusing, and the social prejudice against Blacks was growing. The cold climate, the broken promises, and the hostile environment were discouraging.

Some Blacks united behind Thomas Peters, the former slave from North Carolina who had fought as a sergeant with the Black Pioneers. After struggling unsuccessfully to help his followers attain their land claims, he travelled to England and demanded that they all be sent back to Africa, even though half of them had been born in North America. The British government was sympathetic to his pleas. It granted him and his followers free passage to the British colony of Sierra Leone, which had been established in West Africa by Black Loyalists from England in 1787.

In 1792, one-third of the Black Loyalists in Nova Scotia, 734 adults and 456 children, boarded 15 ships to make the exodus. The rough ocean voyage killed 65 of them. The survivors arrived and built a new settlement called Freetown, which became West Africa's largest coastal city.

First Black Woman in Upper Canada?

Seven-year old Sophia and her sister were the children of slaves in New York State. One day their master's two sons-in-law grabbed the girls, who were playing outside, gagged them with handkerchiefs, threw them in a ship's dark hold, and sailed to Niagara.

Sophia later claimed that she was the first Black girl brought to Canada. She said that she was sold to the famous Native chief and Loyalist, Joseph Brant. He treated her well, but he resold her when she was about 12.

When Governor Simpson's abolition laws came into effect in Upper Canada, Sophia was set free. She moved to Waterloo where she married a Black man named Robert Pooley.

North America's First Policewoman

Little Rose Fortune was about 10 years old when she arrived in a tall ship at Annapolis Royal, Nova Scotia, in 1783. She had been born a slave in Virginia. Her owners, the Devone family, were Loyalists, and they came with their slaves, including Rose and her parents, to relocate in Nova Scotia. After their arrival, Rose and her family were granted their freedom.

Rose became a legend in Nova Scotia and an example of a woman liberated not only from slavery, but from female stereotypes. To support herself, she became a dock worker or "baggage smasher." She carted luggage for arriving passengers from the boats to their homes or hotels. Although very short, Rose was physically strong and able to load and push the baggage in her wheelbarrow. She was an entrepreneur and offered her services to anyone who needed goods transported. She also offered a "wake up" service for people who had to catch a boat or keep an appointment. Her successful business, started about 1825, was the first moving company in Canada. Her descendants are still in the moving business today.

Rose's appearance was unique and unforgettable: her petticoat dangled from under her dress; she wore a man's waistcoat and an apron on top of her dress; on her head was a woman's lace cap crowned with a man's straw hat. The heels on her men's boots made her stand several inches taller. She became a style setter as other Black pioneer women copied her attire.

Rose saw that teenage thugs were a problem on the dock. She elected herself policewoman for the port of Annapolis Royal. The delinquents were soon avoiding her attacks and spankings. Newspapers in Britain wrote about the Black woman who walked the streets as Canada's first policewoman, imposing and enforcing curfews to protect visitors and citizens. Later, Rose joined the Underground Railroad. She transported refugees from the docks to safe houses. Rose Fortune died in 1864 at the age of 90.

Returned to Slavery

Some stories of Black refugees did not have happy endings. Mary Postell was born the slave of a rebel officer but escaped to aid the British in the American Revolution. She worked hard building forts and received her certificate of freedom from the British. When the war ended, an unknown official demanded to see her certificate. It was never returned to her.

She went to Florida to work as a servant for Jesse Gray, but he enslaved her again. When Gray arrived as a Loyalist in Nova Scotia, he brought her and her daughters with him. In Shelburne, she took her children and ran away because she feared that Jesse would sell her and she would be separated from her daughters. But they were soon discovered in Birchtown. In the court case that followed, two Blacks verified Mary's story, but prejudice against slaves escaping from Loyalist masters was strong. White hoodlums burned the homes and killed one of the children of a Black witness.

Gray, who claimed he had lost the original bill of sale for Mary, won the court case and then promptly sold Mary for 100 bushels of potatoes to William Maugham, who lived down the coast in Argyle. Gray kept one of Mary's daughters, Nell, as his slave and sold the other daughter, Flora, to John Henderson.

Colouring Black Heritage

The images in this book have been created by artist A.G. Smith. You may photocopy and colour them to create your own Black heritage portraits.

What you need:
- a photocopy machine
- coloured pencils, crayons, or paint and paint brushes

What to do:
1. Photocopy the page or pages from this book that you wish to colour. Use full-page images, such as those found at the beginning of each chapter. Or you may want to draw your own images.
2. Colour the pictures of your choice.
3. You might decide to frame the pictures or collect a series of them in a book of Black heritage. Create the coloured pictures yourself or with friends or classmates.

CHAPTER 3 *Conductors and Passengers*

Harriet Tubman, Josiah Henson, and Others

The Underground Railroad did not run under the ground and it was not a railroad.

A secret network of whites and free Blacks who were dedicated to helping slaves escape from their masters and reach freedom in the northern states and Canada existed from the 1780s, but the term "Underground Railway" (URR) only became popular about 1840.

The URR had no central command. Individual guides (conductors) used secret codes, signals, messages, and disguises to aid the slaves (passengers). Hidden routes (tracks) zigzagged from one hide-out (station) to the next, often changing direction so as to confuse the hired slave-hunters in hot pursuit. Imagine if you were a passenger, sleeping by day in caves, under bridges, in cellars or barns, walking 50 kilometres by night through hostile towns, wilderness, and swamps. After two or three months of eating leaves or berries, drinking from rivers, surviving rain storms, and shivering on cold nights without shelter, you would hope to reach your destination.

Slavery was legal, and that meant conductors were breaking the law. They could be fined or imprisoned, just as you would be today for aiding an escaped convict. In the southern states, they risked being shot or hanged by plantation owners. Their Christian zeal and belief that slavery was evil encouraged Quakers, Presbyterians, and Wesleyan Methodists to help the fugitives. Free Blacks or former slaves also aided the refugees.

Slavery Abolished in Upper Canada

In 1793, John Graves Simcoe, lieutenant governor of Upper Canada, convinced the Assembly of Upper Canada* to pass an act that made slavery illegal. It did not abolish slavery immediately, as Simcoe wished, but it was the beginning of the end. Any slaves who were brought to Canada or reached Canada by their own efforts would be free immediately. Any children born to slaves after 1793 would be free at the age of 25 and their children would be born free. Slavery was phased out and disappeared entirely by 1820.

Slavery remained legal in the British Empire until 1834 and in the United States until after the Union Army won the Civil War in 1865. Canada was the first haven for slaves in North America. Many slaves in the U.S. heard about freedom in Canada. They risked their lives in attempts to reach Canada, some via the URR and others on their own, using the North Star, which they called "the drinking gourd," to guide them.

The Fugitive Slave Act (1793)

The same year that Simcoe abolished slavery, the Congress of the United States passed the first Fugitive Slave Act, which made it illegal to help or keep a fugitive slave. Escaped slaves in the northern states were no longer safe, and many moved to Canada. The network of honest people who were willing to break the law and aid them grew stronger.

* In 1791, Upper Canada was the present-day province of Ontario; Lower Canada was the present-day province of Quebec. From 1841 to 1867, they were called Canada West and Canada East.

The Fugitive Slave Act (1850)

In the U.S., the differences over slavery became a problem. Plantation owners were unhappy that slaves could escape and live in the northern states. In 1850, southern politicians, protecting the interests of the slave owners, convinced the U.S. Congress to pass a more drastic Fugitive Slave Act. Slave-hunters could pursue, capture, and return a fugitive to a master in the southern states.

Free Blacks were also in danger; they had to prove that they were not escaped slaves. A new slave trade began. Blacks living freely in the northern states were kidnapped by bounty-hunters, who sold them back into slavery. Many more Blacks in the northern states moved to Canada where slavery was illegal.

Some slave-hunters crossed the border and kidnapped Canadian Blacks. Vigilance Committees were formed to watch for them. If they were spotted, alarms sounded. Sometimes mobs of hundreds gathered to stop the kidnappers.

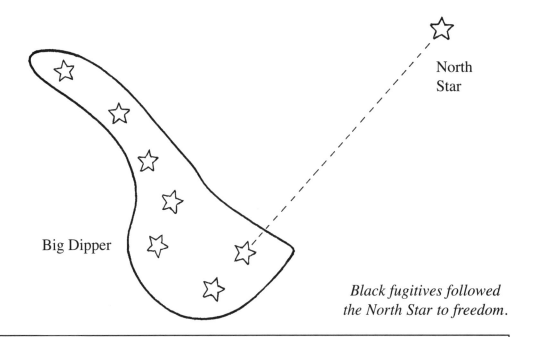

North
Star

Big Dipper

Black fugitives followed
the North Star to freedom.

Secret Railroad Language

Underground Railroad participants used railroad language in written communications or conversations to hide their illegal activities.

Cargo or **Passengers** were terms for the fugitive slaves who were escaping.
Stations or **Depots** were the safe places to stop or rest on the trip north. They might be 40-50 kilometres apart.
Conductors were the people who transported or guided the passengers or cargo.
Agents or **Station Masters** were the volunteers who hid fugitives in their homes, barns, basements, attics, etc.
Employees were the individuals who assisted the slaves in their escape, some for money, others for free. They might be boat operators or real railroad employees who hid the illegal cargo.
Shareholders or **Stockholders** donated the money needed for food, clothing, shelter, or transportation.

White Abolitionists

Slaves had no rights. They could be cruelly chained, beaten, sold without warning, or separated from their families. White abolitionists in Canada and the United States were dedicated to freeing and helping them.

A Quaker woman, Laura Haviland, a school teacher in Windsor, helped slaves in Detroit escape across the river. Another Quaker, Levi Coffin, earned the title President of the Underground Railroad because he saved over 3,500 slaves. He operated in Ohio and Indiana for more than 35 years and built secret hide-outs in his cellars and attics.

Alexander Ross of Belleville, Ontario, was a white medical doctor who hated slavery. His hobby was ornithology, so he would pretend to be studying the local birds on his trips to the southern U.S. in order to conceal the real purpose of his journey, which was to help slaves to escape. He gave them money and supplies, or personally guided them to Canada. In Nashville, a female slave once begged him for help. Her husband had escaped to Canada, and her master was demanding that she remarry. When she objected, she was savagely whipped. Ross dressed her as his male servant and took her to Canada, where he reunited her with her husband.

Ross became famous as a daring abolitionist. During the Civil War, Abraham Lincoln met with Ross and told him about a female Confederate spy in Montreal, code-named Mrs. Williams. The woman was passing on information from southern spies operating in Canada. Ross contacted Mrs. Williams and convinced her that he supported her cause. When he was invited to travel with her on one of her trips to New York, he informed the American police. She was captured at the border with 82 secret messages sewn inside her petticoat.

Thomas Garrett from Philadelphia escorted 2,700 runaways to safety. He was fined so many times that he was left financially broke. As he was paying his last dollars, the person collecting the fine sneered at him: "I hope this cures you of your law breaking." Thomas defiantly answered: "Friend, I haven't a dollar in the world, but if thee knows a fugitive who needs a breakfast, send him to me."

John Fairfield was born into a wealthy slave-owning family, but he opposed slavery. Pretending to be a slave-trader, he travelled south looking for cargo. One day, Fairfield had to transport 28 fugitives past streets full of watchful slave-hunters. He created a phony funeral parade and hid the slaves in the coaches as they snaked slowly past the unsuspecting hunters.

Women agents and conductors were among the most dedicated and daring. One daughter of a tavern owner in Pennsylvania, who was sheltering a female slave, heard the runaway screaming for help. A slave-catcher was kidnapping her. The girl responded quickly. She ran downstairs and attacked the man with a broom until a neighbour arrived and knocked the bounty-hunter unconscious.

An Ohio woman was transporting escapees under a blanket in a wagon but got stuck in a puddle of mud. Four neighbours, who were slave-owners, came to her aid, unaware of her cargo. After much effort, they freed the wagon. She thanked them politely and continued on her way.

Daring Escapes

Disguises were frequently used in the efforts to escape. In 1848, William Craft, a free Black, was determined to rescue his loved one, Ellen, who was a slave. Ellen's skin was light enough for her to pass as a white person. She dressed as a wealthy white man who was travelling north. William posed as her loyal slave and did all the talking for his master, who was too ill to speak. They stayed in the best hotels as they made their way to freedom.

Henry "Box" Brown earned his nickname when he escaped from a

Virginia tobacco company where he was a working slave. With the help of friends, he had himself shipped north in a packing box to the Anti-Slavery Society in Philadelphia. During the 26-hour trip, the box was accidentally turned upside down by railway workers, so he travelled to freedom on his head. When the box was opened, Henry shocked everyone by emerging with the greeting: "How do you do, Gentlemen!"

Burr Plato, a Virginia refugee, escaped with seven other slaves in 1856. He had saved $50, which kept them all alive for more than a month. After reaching freedom at Fort Erie, he had only $5 and a bag of biscuits. In Canada, Burr learned how to read and write, worked hard, saved money for a home, married, and had 10 children. He was one of the first Blacks elected in Canadian municipal politics by white citizens.

Anthony Burns fled from Virginia in 1854 and reached Boston. His owner tracked him down and had him arrested. An angry mob tried to rescue him. As soldiers established order, a participant was killed and others wounded. Days later, the courthouse was chained off as a crowd of 50,000 gathered. Burns was returned to his master, but his supporters raised the money to buy his freedom and send him to college. He became a church pastor, then arrived in Canada and was the minister of the Zion Baptist Church in St. Catharines, Canada West, from 1860 until his death in 1862.

Caught Again

John Mason was a slave in Kentucky until he escaped north to Ohio. Determined to help other Blacks, he returned many times to rescue over 1,300 fellow slaves. On one excursion, he was caught again. The slave-hunters broke both his arms and beat him ruthlessly before selling him back into slavery. He escaped for the second time. Using his Underground Railroad contacts, he reached Hamilton, Ontario, where he made his home.

Josiah Henson

Born a slave on a Maryland plantation in 1789, Josiah experienced the horrors of slavery at a young age. When his father objected to an overseer insulting Josiah's mother, he was whipped with 100 lashes, had his ear cut off, and was sold in the southern states. Then Josiah was separated from his brothers and sisters, as they were all sold to different owners.

When he grew up, Josiah married Charlotte, who was also a slave, and they had 12 children. Because Josiah worked hard and was loyal, his owner put him in charge of the plantation and gave him increased responsibilities. Josiah became a preacher and saved $300 to buy his freedom. But the owner tricked Josiah, who could not read, into signing an agreement that changed the price to $1,000. When he discovered that he was going to be sold, Josiah's anger and fear motivated him to plan a desperate escape.

In 1830, he began the dangerous journey. In a small boat, he rowed his family across the Ohio River. Then Josiah carried his two youngest children in a sack on his back, while the two older ones walked with his wife. The family hid by day and travelled by night, until members of the Underground Railroad helped them finally to reach Canada. He described how he threw himself to the ground in celebration when he reached the shore. He rolled in the sand, kissed the earth, and danced like a madman.

Free at last, in 1849 Josiah created a book about his life titled *The Life of Josiah Henson, Formerly a Slave, Now an Inhabitant of Canada*. Because he could not read or write, Josiah told his story to a friend who wrote it down. The book described his cruel treatment and hard life as a slave. Three years later, Harriet Beecher Stowe wrote a fictional story, based in part on Henson's real-life experiences, called *Uncle Tom's Cabin*. It made Josiah famous and rallied people throughout the world to condemn slavery.

In Canada, Josiah dreamed of an independent settlement for escaping slaves. He risked his own freedom by becoming a conductor on the Underground Railroad and returning to the southern states to escort more than 100 fugitive slaves back to Canada. In 1842, he helped to establish the Dawn Settlement. Josiah continued to preach and give lectures. In 1837, he commanded a Black military company of volunteers who fought and defended Canada. Josiah Henson died in Canada on May 5, 1883.

Harriet Tubman

Harriet Tubman, a slave from Maryland, escaped in 1849 to St. Catharines in Canada West. She had scars on her face and body from childhood beatings. From the age of nine, she worked as a field hand, along with the adult slaves. After being struck on the head by her slave master, Harriet suffered from seizures for the rest of her life.

Harriet earned the biblical nickname "Black Moses" because she returned 19 times to the southern states to escort more than 300 of her people to freedom, including her own parents and three brothers. The small but determined woman would appear without warning, moving quietly, like a ghost. Plantation slaves whispered her name and listened late at night for her song

outside their houses: "When that old chariot comes, who's going with me?" Then they would sing back: "When that old chariot comes, I'm going with you." She brought food and medical supplies, and would carry people too weak to walk. Harriet also carried a pistol, and to anyone ready to give up the journey, she said: "Live North or die here!"

Legends grew about Harriet. Slave owners placed a "Dead or Alive" bounty of $40,000 on her head. On one trip, she was disguised as an elderly woman carrying live chickens, which were flapping on the end of a piece of rope tied around their feet. Suddenly, her former master appeared on the street. Thinking quickly, she let the birds free and chased after them. Not realizing who she really was, everyone laughed at the awkward old lady pursuing the scattering, clucking chickens.

The daring little conductor reportedly claimed: "My train never went off the track, nor did I ever lose a passenger."

When the American Civil War was declared in 1861, Harriet returned to the U.S. and joined the Union Army as a scout and a spy, as well as a nurse. After the war, she lived in the U.S. until her death in 1913.

"The Free Slave"

The following song was written by an American abolitionist, George W. Clarke. As it spread orally through the ranks of the escaping slaves, it took on many different verses and versions.

I'm on my way to Canada
That cold and distant land
The dire effects of slavery
I can no longer stand –

Farewell, old master,
Don't come after me.
I'm on my way to Canada
Where coloured men are free.

36

Mythical Railroad

Many people in the 1800s who heard about the Underground Railroad imagined that a mythical, supernatural train roared through dark underground tunnels far below the surface of the earth, spitting out smoke and fire as it carried fugitives from the American south to freedom in Canada.

The term "Underground Railroad" reportedly was created in the early 1840s by a plantation owner who was puzzled by the rapid and mysterious disappearance of the fugitive slaves he was pursuing. In disgust, he gave up the chase and proclaimed: "There must be an underground railroad around here."

Honeymoon Surprise

James Mink, born in Upper Canada, was the first of 11 children. In 1800, his parents were slaves of a Loyalist in Kingston. James became a free and wealthy businessman. His stagecoaches moved mail, people, and sometimes prisoners between Kingston and Toronto. He also owned stables in Toronto.

He wanted his daughter Minnie to marry well, so he offered $10,000 for a "respectable white husband." James Andrews, originally from Yorkshire, England, was attracted by the reward and proposed to Minnie. They were married and left on a honeymoon to the U.S., where Minnie's new husband immediately sold her as a slave. Months later, her father heard about Minnie's fate and rescued her.

Black Code Laws

Some states created laws to capture fugitive slaves, such as Ohio's Black Codes of 1804 and 1807. Even free Blacks had to obtain certificates of freedom, called "freedoms," to be employed. Businesses were fined for hiring Blacks who didn't have one. Free Blacks entering the state had to put up a $500 bond and prove, within only 20 days, that they had an income or money on which to live. They did not have full legal rights. Fines of $100 stopped anyone from hiding or aiding escaped slaves or illegal free Blacks.

Beware of Canadian Cannibals

As word spread in the southern states that freedom for slaves was possible in "the land of promise" far to the north, the alarmed plantation masters invented wild warnings. Slaves were told that Canada was "a barren country where only black-eyed peas can be grown" and that "the Detroit River to Canada is 3,000 miles wide." Canadians were described as cannibals: "They get you up there, fatten you up, and then boil you."

Manumission

Some slave owners granted freedom to their slaves in their wills because they had shown great loyalty, or because they were too old to sell. This freeing of slaves was known as "manumission." For example, Harriet Tubman discovered that her mother had been granted freedom, but because nobody informed her, she was kept in slavery.

Make a Settler's Cabin

When Black settlers arrived in Canada, it was necessary for them to clear land and build a cabin. Follow these instructions to build your own cabin.

What you need:
- scissors
- white glue
- crayons or coloured pencils
- scoring tool (like the point of a compass)

What to do:
1. Photocopy pages 40 and 41. Colour the parts.

2. Cut out the two wall sections. Score along the edge of the tabs, and fold them back. Apply glue only to the tabs. Do not use too much glue or it will seep through and spoil the paper.

3. Cut out the roof section. Score along the centre line, and glue it to the cabin walls.

4. Cut out and assemble the chimney, and glue it to the end wall.

5. Cut out the figures, and attach them to their bases.

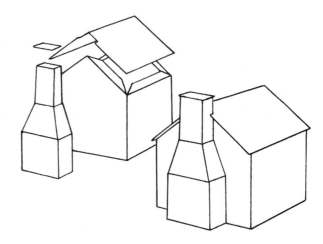

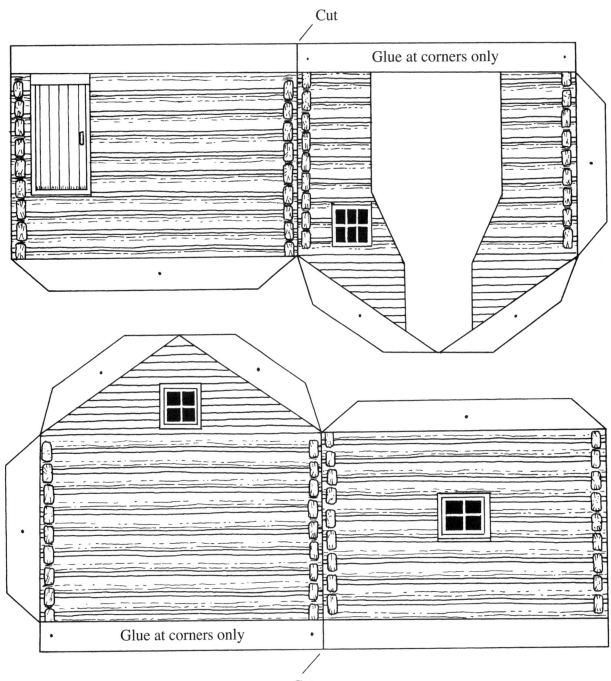

Cut

Glue at corners only

Glue at corners only

Cut

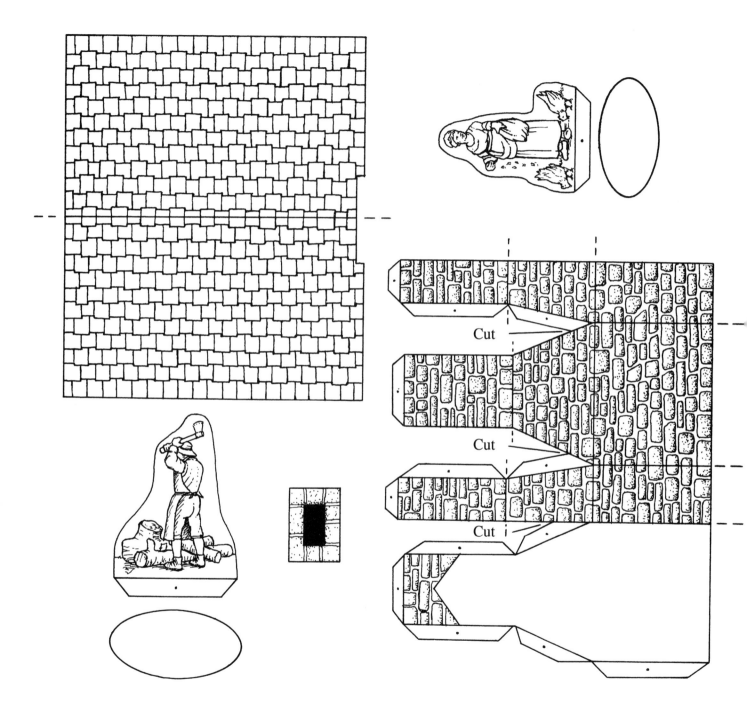

Cut

Cut

Cut

CHAPTER 4 *Early Settlers*

Mary Ann Shadd, Mifflin Gibbs, John Ware, and Others

From the earliest days, Black settlements grew in many parts of present-day Canada.

Before the American Civil War, more than 40,000 Blacks sought refuge in Canada to escape the Fugitive Slave Acts. After the war ended in 1865 and slavery was abolished, more than half of the Black settlers returned to the U.S. Only about 15,000 stayed in Canada.

Henry Bibb

Henry Bibb was born in Kentucky in 1815. His mother was a Black slave, and his father was white. From an early age, Henry was determined to escape what he called "the whips and chains of slavery." In his zeal for freedom, the desperate young rebel escaped from six different masters. His owners frequently resold him. In 1839, Henry stole a horse from his master and boldly posed as a free Black on his escape north to Detroit.

Henry was devoted to helping slaves find shelter, schools, and security in Canada. In 1851, he became the editor of a newspaper, *The Voice of the Fugitive*, in Windsor, Canada West. He also established the Refugee Home Society to create Black communities. White abolitionists supplied financial aid. Henry and his wife, Mary, were placed in charge. The society prospered, grew crops, employed workers, and educated hundreds of students. Families settled on over 100 lots of land. Henry Bibb died in 1854. By 1865, the society had disintegrated, and its members had scattered.

Mary Ann Shadd

Mary Ann Shadd was the eldest of 13 children. She and her brother Isaac came to Canada to escape the Fugitive Slave Acts. Later, her parents, with their younger children, joined her. On one occasion, Mary Ann saw American slave-hunters with a Black boy in Chatham. She snatched the youth from his captors, ran to the courthouse, and rang the bell furiously to alert the whole town. The bounty-hunters quickly disappeared.

At first, Mary Ann was friendly with Henry Bibb, but a bitter rivalry developed when she founded a more radical newspaper, *The Provincial Freeman*, in Windsor to compete with Bibb's *The Voice of the Fugitive*. In those days women weren't employed in the newspaper business. Mary identified herself only as "M. A. Shadd" in her work as writer, editor, and publisher.* *The Provincial Freeman* moved to Toronto, then, in June 1855, to Chatham. She finally revealed that she was a woman. Mary Ann was the first Black woman in North America to be a newspaper editor.

Both newspapers served the Black communities, but Mary Ann confronted and criticized Henry Bibb, who also attacked her. Mary Ann wrote: "Bibb is a dishonest man." Bibb claimed that Mary was descended "from the serpent that beguiled Mother Eve." Mary Ann believed in the integration of Blacks into white society. *The Provincial Freeman* 's motto was "Self-Reliance is the True Road to Independence." Bibb promoted separate Black communities, schools, and churches, subsidized by abolitionists.

In 1859 Abraham D. Shadd, the father of Mary Ann Shadd, became the first Black to be elected to public office in Canada West when he joined the town council of Raleigh.

During the Civil War, Mary Ann returned to the U.S. to fight against

* A friend, Samuel Ringgold Ward, was the official founder. Mary Ann
   had to be a silent partner because she was a woman.

slavery. She became a recruiter in the Union Army, then a school principal, and finally a lawyer in Washington, D.C. Mary Ann Shadd died in 1893.

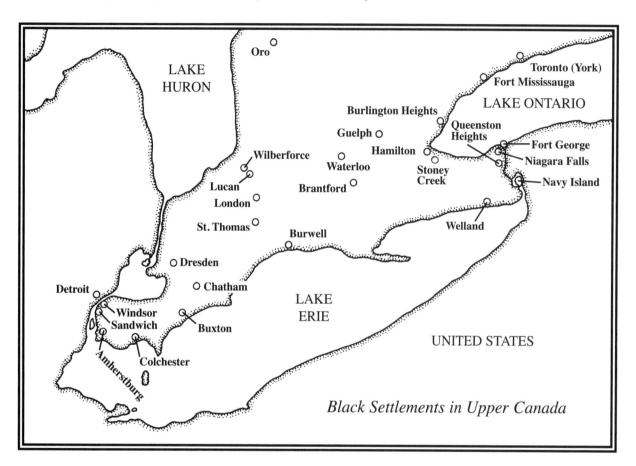

Black Settlements in Upper Canada

Early Upper Canada Settlements

Loyalists in the 1780s, new settlers after the War of 1812, and the Underground Railroad refugees in the mid 1800s brought Black families in large numbers to towns such as Windsor, Chatham, and St. Catharines.

Unsuccessful Settlements

After the War of 1812, many Black communities were created in Upper Canada, but most failed. Sir Peregrine Maitland, the province's first lieutenant governor, created the Oro Settlement near Penetanguishene. By 1840, the village of Edgar was a Black community; by 1848, there were 100 Blacks in Oro. None remained by 1900.

Black businessmen in Cincinnati, Ohio, became fearful of the new Black Code laws of 1807. They purchased land in Lucan, Upper Canada, and promoted the Wilberforce Settlement. By 1832, there were 32 families in the settlement, but poor leadership and corrupt financial problems plagued the sincere efforts of church supporters. It was closed by 1856.

The famous refugee slave, Josiah Henson, with the help of missionaries and generous Quakers from the U.S., created the Dawn Settlement with a school called the British American Institute. It offered practical elementary, industrial, and manual labour courses, along with free room and board. A sawmill was built in 1844 and a gristmill in 1848. It had 70 students and prospered, but then financial problems, legal battles, and leadership changes led to its downfall. The settlement's land and assets were sold in 1872.

In 1845, the African Methodist Episcopal Church created a Black settlement in Sandwich Township near Windsor. It was known as the Coloured Industrial Society. By 1855 it had ended in failure. Henry Bibb's effort to create the Refugee Home Society in 1851 also failed.

Emancipation Day Parades

At midnight on July 31, 1834, Britain officially ended slavery. Blacks in Canada declared August 1 to be Emancipation Day. Black communities celebrated it yearly with a parade of colourful costumes and festivities, which included dinners, speeches, cannon fire, dances, sports events, and music.

The Elgin Settlement

Ironically, it was an Irishman, the Reverend William King, who created Canada West's only successful, self-supporting, all-Black community.

King was born in Ireland in 1812 and educated in Scotland. In 1834, his family moved to Ohio, and he became a teacher in Louisiana. He married Mary Phares, the daughter of a plantation owner. Later, the family moved to Scotland, but tragedy struck. King's wife, daughter, and son all died within two years. King became a minister and went to Canada.

As King was creating a settlement to aid escaped slaves, he suddenly discovered that he was himself a slave-owner! His father-in-law had died and left him 14 slaves. King went to Louisiana, settled the will, and travelled north with his slaves. On the trip, he rescued another Black child. He told the 15 Blacks that they were free but gave them the option of joining his new settlement in Canada. They all chose to join him.

King returned to Canada West and convinced his church to purchase land near Chatham. The plan was to give land grants to Black refugees and teach them to become self-supporting farmers, but King ran into strong opposition. A powerful politician named Edwin Larwill challenged King to a public debate in Chatham. King was warned by the sheriff that his life was in danger if he participated. A crowd of over 300, who feared the Black community, booed and shouted when King began to speak.

King became so unpopular in Chatham that, after one late-night church meeting, he had to be guarded by a silent crew of 12 armed Black men, who escorted him back to his hotel. Larwill attempted to stop the Blacks from attending public schools and voting. He suggested they be charged bond money, similar to some of the Black Codes in the U.S. King became more determined, and on November 28, 1849, he opened the Elgin Settlement, whose first residents were the 15 slaves he had freed.

The Amherstburg Church

Buxton Mission School

In 1850, the Elgin Association was formed with a board of 24 directors to manage the settlement. Also, the Buxton Mission was created by the Presbyterian Church to supply a chapel and school to the refugees. King offered his own money to help finance them. They were built as the core of the Elgin Settlement, which soon expanded to include a sawmill, gristmill, brickyard, store, and pearl-ash factory.

The education at the Buxton Mission School was superior, and its reputation soon attracted outsiders. By 1854, half the students were white. The people of Chatham saw the achievements of their new neighbours. The prejudice based on false fears disappeared. The all-Black Elgin Settlement was a success due to the hard work and the good character of its citizens.

Lower Canada Settlement

Today, the only remains of a Black settlement in Lower Canada are the ruins of a stone chapel built in 1831. Using the North Star for navigation, Blacks followed Lake Champlain and river routes to establish a community of workers and tradespeople at Moore's Corner* in the 1790s. Their graves in the local cemetery have since been bulldozed.

Early British Columbia Settlements

In the 1850s, California initiated its own version of the Fugitive Slave Act. Blacks could not testify in a court of law against a white person. If accused by a slave-hunter of being a runaway, they could not defend themselves. Also, their children could not go to state schools, and Blacks had to register to work. The California State Legislature took away their civil rights.

California Blacks were free, educated people, not illiterate refugees. Some were rich landowners and businessmen; others were teachers, barbers, bakers, or tailors. When the governor of Victoria in British Columbia assured them that they would be accepted and treated equally, about 800 Blacks left California to go to Victoria in 1858. They settled along the coast of the British Columbia mainland and on Saltspring Island.

The Blacks came at the right time. Gold had been discovered! Thousands of new immigrants were searching for instant wealth. The province was booming with people buying land, building homes, and opening stores. Many Blacks became police officers in Victoria and later formed British Columbia's first militia unit in 1860, the all-Black Victoria Pioneer Rifle Company, also called the African Rifles. It was the colony's only protection against the threat of American expansion or invasion, which was a strong possibility at the time because the majority of the fortune-seekers in the gold rush were from California.

* Present-day St.-Armand, Quebec.

Mifflin Gibbs

Mifflin Wistar Gibbs arrived in 1858 and opened many businesses in Victoria. In California, he had owned stores that sold clothing and shoes. In British Columbia, he supplied groceries and tools to gold miners. He was soon wealthy. In 1866, he was elected to the city council in Victoria. He managed the city's finances. In 1871, he encouraged British Columbia to join Canada. Mifflin Gibbs returned to the U.S., was made a judge, and later was sent to Africa as America's official representative in Madagascar.

Cowboy John Ware

In 1882, a large and powerful Texas cowboy moved to the present-day prairie province of Alberta. John Ware had been born a slave, but was freed after slavery was abolished in 1865. Although many Blacks were returning to the U.S. at the time, he did the opposite and came to settle in Canada.

John Ware was an expert gunman and could tame wild horses. He could lasso cows and wrestle powerful bulls to the ground. He was one of the pioneers of the western rodeo, and frequently collected prize money for his riding and roping skills. A few years after John drove a herd of longhorn cattle to the Canadian West, he married Mildred Lewis and they brought up five children. John Ware met a cowboy's fate in 1905 when his galloping horse stumbled in a prairie hole. As the two of them collapsed and rolled to the hard ground, the horse landed on top of John and killed him.

The Black Trek

After Oklahoma became a state in 1907, it created many laws that were prejudiced against Blacks. Many began the Black Trek. About 1,000 Black farmers and ranchers migrated to Alberta, Saskatchewan, and Manitoba. Others settled in the cities. By 1911, there were approximately 150 Blacks in

Winnipeg, 150 in Vancouver, and 300 in Edmonton. For example, Mattie Mayes, a Black woman and former slave from Georgia, came in 1910 with her husband to Saskatchewan to settle near North Battleford. Joe Mayes became the first pastor of the church congregation.

Unfortunately, discrimination also spread to Canada. In 1911, when fearful Canadian bureaucrats heard that even greater numbers of Oklahoma Blacks were preparing to travel north, they became alarmed. Canadian law prevented anyone from stopping the immigrants because of their race, so the officials were secretly ordered to refuse them for medical reasons.

The Walking Newspaper

John "Daddy" Hall was born in Amherstburg, Upper Canada, about 1807. His parents, who were of Black and Native heritage, had 11 children. When John was very young, American bounty-hunters raided the community and kidnapped him, his mother, and all his brothers and sisters. They were dragged south to Kentucky and sold to different plantation masters.

John grew up and fell in love with a young female slave. Together, they planned an escape. After a dangerous trek, avoiding slave-hunters and surviving in the harsh countryside, they eventually reached Toronto.

When his wife died, John remarried four times. His fifth wife was from England. He fathered a total of 10 children. In 1843, John became the first Black resident of Sydenham, near Owen Sound. By 1851, he was the town's night watchman. He was also the town crier. He roamed the streets ringing his bell and making public announcements. During 50 years as town crier, John became famous as the "walking newspaper" of Owen Sound. When he died in 1925, the legendary old man was said to be 118 years old.

In a desperate attempt to reach freedom, Charles Mitchell, a Black slave boy, hid himself on an American ship going to Canada. Out on the Pacific Ocean, he was discovered and dragged before the captain, who locked him up and intended to return the frightened youngster to his master.

In September 1860, the ship arrived at Victoria, British Columbia, where local Blacks heard about the captive. A sheriff, responding to their complaints, boarded the ship and, ignoring the captain's screaming objections, rescued the youth. After a judge set him free, Charles was allowed to go to school in his new Victoria home.

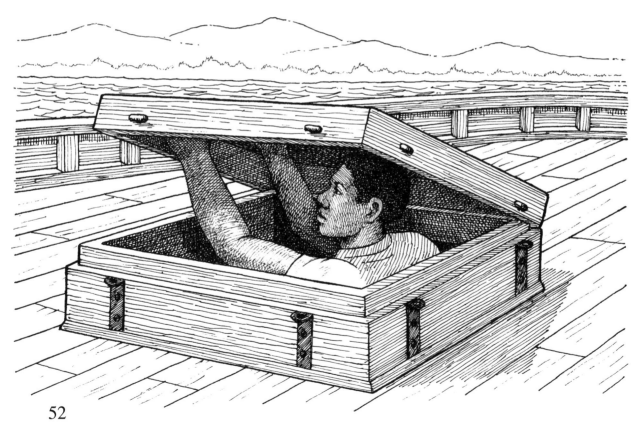

Doc Butler

Peter Bowzer was born a slave in Maryland in 1797, but he escaped and became a sailor. To hide from his past, he changed his name to Butler.

He returned from his sea adventures, married a Native woman called Salome Squawker, and started a family. In 1829, they moved to Upper Canada and joined the Wilberforce Settlement where they farmed and raised seven children. Peter became the treasurer of the settlement in 1836, and the "doctor" of Wilberforce. His famous herbal medicines cured many Blacks and whites. Peter was also a natural businessman and bought up land around the town of Lucan until his estate was worth a fortune.

Peter the III

The grandson of Doc Butler, like his father and grandfather, was named Peter. He was born in Lucan in 1859 and became famous as its large, Black police officer. In 1883, he became a Middlesex County policeman and, 30 years later in 1913, a member of the Ontario Provincial Police.

He was a sharp shooter and owned over 38 guns that he had taken from criminals, including the infamous Irish clan from Lucan known as the Black Donnellys. Yet he rarely carried a gun. He patrolled the streets toting a large stick and enforced the law with his powerful fists. Whites and Blacks, cattle rustlers, and honest citizens respected and feared him, but he was an understanding man who treated the prisoners in his jail to a bucket of beer on Saturday night and offered unemployed tramps food and the opportunity to work on his farm for cash.

CHAPTER 5 *Soldiers*

Richard Pierpoint, U.E., William Hall, V.C., and Others

Blacks have fought for our country with courage and bravery throughout Canada's history.

Black Loyalist soldiers were among the first to settle in Canada in 1776. In 1812, the Americans declared war on Britain and invaded Canada. Determined to protect their new homes, Black Loyalists quickly grabbed their weapons, eager to defend Canada and their own freedom.

Richard Pierpoint, U.E.

Richard Pierpoint was born in Bondou, Africa. At the age of 16, he was kidnapped by slave-traders. He survived the long, cruel voyage across the Atlantic Ocean shackled in the dark hold of a slave ship and, in 1760, was sold in America to a British army officer. His loyal service to the British during the American Revolution as a member of Butler's Rangers earned him his freedom and the title of United Empire Loyalist.* He was one of the 10 Black Loyalists who arrived in Upper Canada in 1780.

In 1812, Blacks fought in many regiments from Upper Canada, but Richard Pierpoint created Canada's first all-Black company of soldiers, Robert Runchey's Company of Coloured Men. The white commander, Robert Runchey, was officially in charge, but it was Pierpoint who had the idea for the special company, and it was he who inspired and led the men. They

* United Empire Loyalists, and all their descendants today, have the honour and privilege of placing "U.E." after their names.

helped to win the Battle of Queenston Heights and fought in other battles and encounters in the war.

In his old age, Pierpoint asked the British government to finance his return to Africa, but instead he accepted a land grant near Fergus, Ontario, where he died and was buried in 1837. Today, a plaque in St. Catharines, Ontario, honours his memory and service to Canada.

The Jamaican Maroons

In July 1796, the Jamaican Maroons arrived in Halifax. They were 600 strong, military resistance fighters who were both respected and feared. Originally slaves from Africa, they had escaped from their masters in 1655, taken up arms, and lived in the hills and mountains of Jamaica for more than 100 years, resisting all efforts to recapture them.

They arrived as free Blacks, were employed to build the Citadel in Halifax, and given food, houses, and clothing. They formed an independent militia unit with their own leaders as officers. Their combat experience gave the local citizens a sense of protection, but they were carefully watched by the uneasy authorities because of their reputation as violent guerrilla fighters. They completed the construction of the Citadel, but disliked the cold, harsh Canadian weather and asked to be sent to a warmer place. In August 1800, 550 of them departed for Sierra Leone in Africa.

The Mackenzie Rebellion

When William Lyon Mackenzie attempted to overthrow the government of Upper Canada in 1837, his rebellion failed because of the loyalty of the majority of the citizens, but no group was more loyal or determined to defeat his rebels than the Black citizens. They regarded Mackenzie's American-style democracy and his support from his friends in the U.S. as a threat to their freedom, because slavery still existed in the United States.

Jamaican Maroons building the Citadel in Halifax

In December 1837, Captain James Sears formed a company of 50 Blacks to fight the rebels, and Hugh Eccles commanded another Black unit at Niagara. In Windsor, Josiah Henson commanded yet another company of Black volunteers, which was part of the Essex Militia that captured the rebel schooner *Anne*, taking the crew as prisoners. Henson's Black unit defended Fort Malden along with another company of 123 Black volunteers known as Captain Caldwell's Coloured Corps. Blacks in Hamilton formed a company commanded by Captain Allan. There were two Black companies of militiamen from Chatham. All bravely defended Canada from the rebels.

William Hall, V.C.

Queen Victoria ruled Great Britain from 1837 to 1901. She created a special military medal, the Victoria Cross, which was given only to the bravest members of the armed forces of the British Empire who performed daring feats during battle. The first medals were awarded in 1857. Since then, it has been awarded to only 1,355 people, including 94 Canadians.

In 1857, the first Canadian sailor and the first Black to be given the honour was William Hall. William was the son of an escaped slave from Virginia who reached freedom in Nova Scotia in 1814. William was born in 1827, and at the age of 12, he went to sea to become a sailor.

In 1852, he began a distinguished career in the Royal Navy. He served on Lord Nelson's famous flagship, *Victory*. During the Crimean War in 1853, he received medals at the Battle of Inkerman and the siege of Sebastopol. He was serving on the frigate *Shannon*, which was sent to Calcutta when the Indian mutiny broke out in 1857. The captain ordered William and 409 others to travel overland to Lucknow, India, where the British commander was attempting to survive against an army of mutineers.

His commander asked for volunteers to join a gun crew that would try to break through the walls of the fortress temple of Shah Nejeef. They had to volunteer because it was considered a suicide mission. All the gun crew were killed, except for Hall and his badly wounded lieutenant. Nevertheless, William continued to load and fire the gun, ignoring bullets whizzing past him, until he finally blew a hole through the wall. That made it possible for British soldiers to conquer the stronghold. For his bravery, Able Seaman William Hall received the Victoria Cross.

After 23 years, William retired from the Royal Navy and returned to Nova Scotia. He died in 1904, and the Canadian Legion built a monument to his memory in 1947.

John Brown and Harper's Ferry
The famous American abolitionist, John Brown, a white man with a long flowing beard, was an anti-slavery fanatic, who claimed he had been appointed by God to free the slaves. He and his enthusiastic supporters would strike suddenly, attacking plantations and rescuing slaves, who often joined the cause.

On October 16 in 1859, Brown conducted a daring attack on the American arsenal at Harper's Ferry in West Virginia. Twenty-one men joined Brown on the raid. Brown and five others were captured and hanged for treason.

Ten died during the attack, and six escaped. Brown became a hero and martyr who symbolized the Black quest for freedom. A few years later, the American Civil War erupted, and Union soldiers marching south to free the slaves sang: "John Brown's body lies a-mouldering in the grave," but "His truth goes marching on."

In 1858, Brown had come to Canada West with 13 dedicated followers to plan and train for the raid at Harper's Ferry. Chatham, the last stop for many Blacks seeking freedom via the Underground Railroad, had a strong Black community. Many of Chatham's Black leaders sympathized with and supported Brown's cause; others feared his revolutionary ideas.

John Brown

At a meeting in Chatham, Brown and his followers adopted The Provisional Constitution and Ordinances for the People of the United States. The Shadd family gave Brown the use of their newspaper offices and printing press. Many Blacks in Canada prepared to travel to the United States and join his revolution. One Canadian, Osborne Perry Anderson, was elected as a congressman in Brown's provisional government and participated in the attack on Harper's Ferry. He survived the disaster and later wrote a book, *A Voice From Harper's Ferry*, with Mary Ann Shadd.

American Civil War, 1861–1865

When the American Civil War was declared, many Black refugees living in Canada returned to the U.S. to fight against the south. There were many causes of the war, but the main objective of Blacks was to end slavery.

Before the Civil War, 40,000 Blacks had come to

Osborne Anderson

Canada, but some of Canada's most prominent Black settlers, such as Harriet Tubman, Mifflin Gibbs, and Mary Ann Shadd, returned to the U.S. when slavery ended.

Martin Delany, the first Black to graduate from Harvard University in the

U.S., arrived in Chatham in 1856 as a doctor. He became a strong supporter of Chatham's Black community and a political organizer. He wrote editorials for Mary Ann Shadd's newspaper, *The Provincial Freeman*. When John Brown arrived in town, Delany supported his cause.

During the American Civil War, Dr. Delany met with President Abraham Lincoln and impressed him so much that he was made a major in the Union Army, the highest rank given to any Black. He created the 104th Regiment of Colored Troops and encouraged Black Canadians to join it. Forty Blacks from the Elgin Settlement enlisted. Abraham W. Shadd, a younger brother of Mary Ann Shadd, had already returned to join the 55th Massachusetts, but Delany made him a captain in his new regiment.

Other Wars

Since Confederation in 1867, Black Canadians have been a part of our proud military tradition in all the wars or conflicts in which Canadian troops have fought, including W.W.I, W.W.II, Korea, Bosnia, Iraq, and Afghanistan. Canadian soldiers have served also as peacekeepers with United Nations forces. Many have lost their lives, including Corporal Ainsworth Dyer, who was one of four Canadian troops killed by "friendly fire" from an American pilot in Afghanistan in 2002.

Black Warriors

Robert Runchey's Company of Coloured Men was not the only Black unit to fight at Queenston Heights. Joseph Brant, who brought his nation of Loyalist Mohawks to live on the Grand River Reserve after the American Revolution, was himself the owner of 30 to 40 Black slaves, but that did not prevent him in the 1790s from allowing dozens of free Black refugees to take shelter, live with, and marry among the Mohawks on their reserve. Joseph's 18-year-old son, John Brant, arrived at the Battle of Queenston Heights in command of 140 Native and about 50 Black warriors from the reserve to help win the victory over the invading American army.

White Prophet

A white Canadian abolitionist named Stewart Taylor also joined John Brown's raid on Harper's Ferry. He told others that he had experienced a strange, supernatural premonition or dream that he would die during the attack. He was one of the 10 who were killed.

Canada's Best Kept Military Secret

A book written by Calvin Rusk, *The Black Battalion, 1916–1920: Canada's Best Kept Military Secret*, describes the role of some Black Canadians in World War I. Blacks served alongside other Canadians throughout the army during the war, but the No. 2 Construction Battalion was an all-Black labour battalion of 600 soldiers. Ruck claims that "Canadians of all races have no idea that Blacks served, fought, bled, and died" for their country.

Create and Award a Medal

Soldiers are awarded medals for outstanding bravery in battle. You can create and award a medal to a deserving person.

What you need:
- bristol board
- 10 cm of wide ribbon
- 10 cm of thin wire
- a safety pin

- white glue
- scissors
- crayons, coloured pencils, or markers

What to do:
1. From the bristol board, cut out two shapes of the same size. They can be circles, squares, hexagons, etc. Decorate one of the shapes to create your medal.
2. Make a loop from a 5 or 6 cm piece of fine wire.
3. Apply glue to the back of one shape. Place the loop of wire as shown, and press the two shapes together.
4. Make a loop with a wide ribbon and glue the ends together.
5. Cut two short strips of bristol board and glue them inside the ribbon.
6. Make a small hole in the bottom of the ribbon, and insert a small piece of wire. Loop it through the wire in the medal, and join it in the back of the ribbon.
7. Attach a safety pin to the back of the ribbon. Award your medal!

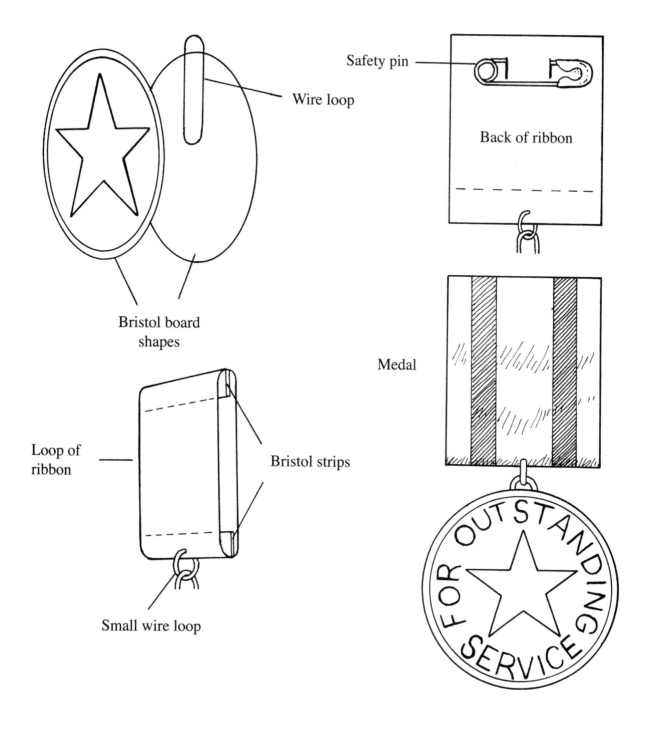

Wire loop

Bristol board shapes

Loop of ribbon

Bristol strips

Small wire loop

Safety pin

Back of ribbon

Medal

FOR OUTSTANDING SERVICE

CHAPTER 6 *Trailblazers*

Anderson Abbott, Herb Carnegie, Elijah McCoy, and Others

Black Canadians often faced social prejudice and unique hardships as slaves and servants, but their daring achievements and huge contributions to our country, and the world, are amazing.

Many individual Black trailblazers made spectacular inroads in all professions and aspects of Canadian life in the past. Today, Black citizens continue to make new and unique contributions.

Black Businessman

Wilson Ruffin Abbott was born a free Black in Virginia in 1801. At the age of 15, he ran away from his home and worked at various labour jobs in hotels and on a Mississippi steamboat. On the boat, the youth fell in love with a Black maid, Ellen Toyer, and the young couple married. They moved to Mobile, Alabama, where Wilson opened a general store.

Unexpectedly, the city passed new laws forcing free Blacks to wear a badge to verify that they were bonded. Two white men would have to guarantee that Wilson was of good character. He ignored the insulting new rules, but immediately received threats that his store would be attacked.

Wilson quickly emptied his bank account and sent his wife and children to safety in New Orleans. As predicted, his store was raided and all his property destroyed. He could not obtain compensation for the destruction. Wherever they moved in the U.S., the Abbotts encountered prejudice. They moved to Toronto in 1835 and prospered. By 1875, they owned more than 75 properties from Toronto to Hamilton. Wilson's wife, Ellen, created the Queen Victoria Benevolent Society to aid other new refugees.

Canada's First Black Doctor

The Abbotts' five daughters and four sons received a good education at the Buxton School in Elgin. One son, Anderson R. Abbott, was born in Toronto in 1837, the same year his father joined Captain Fuller's Company to help defeat the Mackenzie Rebellion.

Dr. A.R. Abbott

Anderson graduated from the University of Toronto in 1857, at the age of 23, and became the first Canadian-born Black doctor. When the American Civil War was declared, he was one of eight Black surgeons in the Union Army. He was put in charge of hospitals in Washington. After the war, he practised in Chatham, Dundas, Oakville, and Toronto. He returned to New York to serve on the staff of the Commanding Officers Department and later was medical superintendent of a hospital in Chicago. Before he returned to Toronto, he was so well respected in the U.S. that the wife of President

Lincoln personally presented him with the shawl that her assassinated husband had worn to his first inauguration.

Canada's First Black Lawyer

Delos Rogest Davis was born in Colchester Township near Amherstburg in 1846, where he was a school teacher for four years. By the age of 25, his talents had led to his appointment as commissioner of affidavits.

Delos wanted to be a lawyer, but at that time no Black person had become a lawyer anywhere in Canada. He completed the difficult law course. Next, he had to work for an existing law firm (article under another lawyer) and finally pass the Bar examination to become a certified lawyer.

Prejudice was strong enough that, despite all his efforts, no white lawyers or law firms would allow him to work for them. In desperation, Delos asked the Ontario Legislature to force the Supreme Court of Judicature to change its rules and allow him to pay the fee and take the Bar examination without first articling. In 1884, the legislature agreed and, in 1885, he became Canada's first Black lawyer. In 1910, Delos was appointed Canada's first Black King's Counsel.

Early Toronto Politician

Today, the corner of Bloor Street and Brunswick Avenue is in the middle of Toronto, Canada's largest city. In the 1840s, it was a lonely cabin in the woods and the home of a Black family named Hubbard. The father, who was a refugee from Virginia, worked as a hotel waiter in Niagara Falls.

In the 1860s, his son, William Hubbard, drove a horse-drawn taxicab for an uncle who owned a livery stable. On a brisk winter day, the young man was travelling along Don Mills Road when he witnessed an accident involving another cab. The horse and vehicle were about to fall into the cold Don River below. Acting quickly, William saved the passenger from falling, possibly to his death. The man turned out to be George Brown, editor of the *Globe* newspaper and a politician. In fact, Brown later became one of Canada's Fathers of Confederation. Brown was so grateful that he made William Hubbard his personal driver.

William married, raised a family, opened a bakery business, and invented and sold his own ovens. By the age of 51, he was a wealthy and successful citizen and took the advice of his friend George Brown, who encouraged him to enter politics. William was elected alderman in Toronto in 1894, and again in the next 13 elections. He became a major Toronto politician, second only to the mayor, and held many important jobs. Throughout his life, he supported the Black community and church.

Doc Shadd

Alfred Shadd, born in 1870, was the son of Mary Ann Shadd's younger brother Garrison. He taught at the Buxton Mission School in Chatham.

When Alfred was 26 years old, he had a thirst for adventure that took him to Canada's frozen North-West Territories to teach in Kinistino. When he arrived, a small, curious female pupil, who had never before seen a Black person, tried to wipe the black off his face. Alfred only smiled kindly and explained that it was a permanent colour.

Alfred loved the North and remained there most of his life. In 1905, Saskatchewan became a province and Shadd ran in the first provincial election. He lost by only 54 votes, but became known as the first Black person to attempt to become a provincial politician.

Although not successful politically, Alfred did carve a name for himself in the North. He studied medicine at the University of Toronto and became a doctor. He was also a farmer, a businessman, a member of the Anglican Church, and the owner and writer of a local newspaper.

Doc Shadd became a northern legend. He travelled long distances, often through heavy snowstorms, to serve patients. On one occasion, he reportedly helped a farm woman to give birth, then went out to the family barn to deliver a new calf. On his death in 1915, people in Saskatchewan overflowed the church in honour of his many contributions to them.

The Real McCoy

The expression "The Real McCoy" is used today throughout the world to describe any product of high-quality that is authentic, original, or unique. It was first used to describe the inventions of a Black trailblazer named Elijah McCoy, who was born in Colchester, Canada West, on May 2, 1844.

Elijah's parents, former slaves from Kentucky, had escaped to Canada via the Underground Railroad. Young Elijah always loved taking things apart and putting them back together. He had the natural curiosity of a mechanical engineer. Blacks were not admitted to engineering schools in North America, so his parents saved their money and sent him to school in Scotland when he was 15. He graduated as a master mechanic and engineer, then returned to North America just after the Civil War. But, because of racist attitudes, no one would hire a Black engineer.

Elijah had to settle for a job as a fireman/oilman on the Michigan Central Railroad. He shovelled coal into the steam-powered locomotive, and every few miles the train stopped so that he could lubricate the engine and walk the length of the train to apply oil to the axles and bearings.

It was not long before Elijah's creative mind and engineering talent designed a solution to prevent the overheating and eliminate the frequent stops. In 1872, he invented and patented a lubricating cup. It dripped oil automatically, as needed, while the train was moving. Because it saved time and money, it was instantly demanded by all railroads. Others copied it, but many buyers insisted on "the real McCoy."

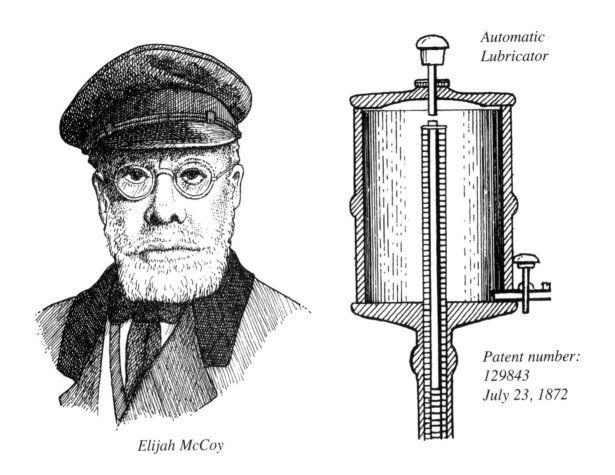

Automatic
Lubricator

Patent number:
129843
July 23, 1872

Elijah McCoy

Elijah obtained financial backing, built a workshop, created new mechanical inventions, and continued to improve his lubricating cup. Soon, variations of it were lubricating engines in cars, ships, factories, mining equipment, oil-drilling rigs, and on construction sites. In total, he registered 58 or more patents that were used throughout the world. In 1916, he perfected the graphite lubricator to oil the new superheater trains. In 1920, he established the Elijah McCoy Manufacturing Company.

Today, we take for granted many of his inventions. When his wife needed an easier way to iron clothes, he invented and patented a portable ironing board. When he grew tired of watering the lawn by hand, he invented the lawn sprinkler.

He and his wife, Mary Eleanor Delany, lived in Detroit, Michigan, for 50 years, until a tragic automobile accident killed her in 1922. Her death affected Elijah's health until his death in 1929.

Little Chocolate

Little George Dixon was only 16 when he knocked out Young Johnson in round three of a bare-fisted boxing match in his home town of Halifax. By the time he turned 17, he had moved to Boston to become a professional boxer.

In 1890, George was matched against a well-known New York boxer, Cal McCarthy, at Washington Hall in Boston. The two young men, wearing 57 gram gloves, fought 70 gruelling rounds in four hours and forty minutes and ended in a draw. But Dixon became famous and earned his affectionate nickname, Little Chocolate, as a result of the match.

The next year, in England, he knocked out Nunc Wallace to become the World Bantamweight Champion and the first Black boxer to win a world boxing championship. Then, on July 8, 1891, he moved up to the featherweight division and knocked out Australia's Abe Attell after only five rounds to become the World Featherweight Champion. He fought off all challengers for six years, until he lost the title in 1897. But the next year he won it back and held onto it until 1900.

George Dixon was called "the greatest little fighter the black race has ever produced," yet he died in such poverty that his friends had to raise money for his burial.

George Dixon

Other Black Trailblazers

1918: John Robinson organized the first Black union, Order of Sleeping Car Porters.

1932: Ray Lewis from Hamilton, Ontario, a railway porter, won a bronze medal as a member of the 4 x 400-metre relay team at the Los Angeles Olympics.

1946: Herb Trawick was Canada's first Black professional football player.

1948: Ruth Bailey and Gwennyth Barton became Canada's first Black nurses.

1951: Rev. Addie Aylestock was the first ordained Black woman.

1954: Violet King became the first Black female lawyer.

1955: Lt. Colonel Ken Jacobs became Canada's first Black Flying Officer.

1967: Toronto's Black community created Caribana. Other Canadian cities followed the example.

1987: Pamela Appelt, scientist turned artist, named the first Black female judge of the Court of Canadian Citizenship.

1991: Julius Alexander Isaac, born in Grenada, appointed Chief Justice of the Federal Court of Canada.

Canada's All-Black Line

From an early age, Herbert Carnegie dreamed of playing in the National Hockey League. He once claimed, "If a puck was edible, I would have had it for breakfast, dinner and supper." Herb was born in Toronto in 1919 and, as a teenager, he displayed amazing talent. The fast-moving young forward played in Quebec for the Sherbrooke Saints. By his early twenties, Herb was the star player in the Quebec Senior Hockey League. The next step in his career should have been the NHL.

Herb reported eagerly to the New York Rangers training camp and impressed all who watched him or played against him. But then came a stunning blow, worse than any heavy check on the ice. He could not play in the NHL because he was Black. It was an unwritten NHL rule of that time.

Shattered, but defiant, Herb returned to play for the Sherbrooke Saints on Canada's first and only all-Black line with his brother Ozzie and Mannie McIntyre. Later, Herb accepted Punch Imlach's offer to join the Quebec Aces, where one of his teammates was Jean Beliveau. Herb outscored the future Montreal Canadiens star for two years, but was left behind as Beliveau progressed to the NHL. According to referee Red Storey, "There are plenty of guys in the Hockey Hall of Fame who couldn't have carried [Herb's] skates."

Herb heard that Conn Smythe, the founder and owner of the Toronto Maple Leafs, had said in a bad joke: "I'll give $10,000 to anyone who can turn Herb Carnegie white!" Herb didn't become bitter, only more determined to fight discrimination. In the 1950s, he became a coach and founded the Future Aces Hockey School, which promoted skill training, team play, and positive self-esteem.

Herb later applied his energy and talents to another game known to exclude Blacks: he became Canada's first Black champion golfer. Carnegie was also a Black trailblazer in the business world. As a stock broker and financial planner, he had a highly successful career for 24 years with the Investors Syndicate. His desire to end prejudice motivated him in 1987 to create the Future Aces Foundation, which stimulates students to use their talents and act to "co-operate and seek understanding with all people, regardless of colour, race or creed."

Jackie Robinson, the first Black baseball player in the major leagues, started his professional career in 1946 playing for the Montreal Royals. Herb had the ability to be the first Black hockey player in the NHL, but racial prejudice prevented it. In his eighties, Herb Carnegie is now blind, but that setback hasn't stopped his motivational talks, scholarship funds, or efforts to shape positive skills for young people.

African Griots

Storytelling has ancient roots in Black culture. In Africa, the griots were the storytellers and historians, men or women, who created stories about the people in their villages and made their living by telling them or singing them at marriages, funerals, or social gatherings. They were the keepers of the oral history. They had no books, videos, films, CDs, or DVDs to pass on their creations. When they died, the stories and the history died with them. Today, dancing, singing, and storytelling remain a Black tradition for sharing pain or happiness.

Tell a Story or Sing a Song

Like a griot, create a story, song, or poem to describe the achievements of a Black individual or a group of Blacks found in this book or elsewhere.

What you need:
- paper and pen or computer to write or print the lyrics
- imagination to create the lyrics
- desire to tell a story about the person or people of your choice

What to do:
1. Decide on the type of story, song, or poem that you wish to create. For a story, you could write a descriptive narrative or a script for a play. For a song, you could sing rap, hip-hop, free-style, folk, or country and western. For a poem, you might try a dub poem, a ballad, a descriptive lyric, or a sonnet.
2. Decide on a topic or theme, such as a specific Black individual, Black achievements, Black pioneers, Black musicians, Black hardships, etc.
3. Research the life of the person or people you have chosen.
4. Create words or lyrics to describe their accomplishments and contributions to Canada or the world.
5. With your friends, you may wish to create or find music to match the words or lyrics and perform the story, poem, or song. You might present it as a live performance, recorded on an audio tape or CD, or on a video tape or DVD.

CHAPTER 7 *New Canadians*

Michaëlle Jean, Grant Fuhr, and Others

By 1921, the majority of the 20,000 Blacks living in Canada had been born here. Most of the others had come from the U.S. Today, the descendants of the early Blacks have been joined by large numbers of new Canadians from Africa, South America, and the Caribbean. They contribute to every aspect of Canadian culture and life. More than 700,000 Blacks now live in Canada.

New Rules and Laws

In the past, Blacks were prevented from belonging to some schools, clubs, churches, professional associations, sports teams, and neighbourhoods. They were frequently limited to lower paying jobs. During the 1950s and 1960s, new laws were introduced in Canada that made it illegal for anyone to refuse employment, service, and housing based on a person's race or religion. Today, education, skills, and abilities determine most people's choices, rather than the colour of their skin.

In 1967, the point system was established for Canadian immigrants; it was thought to be more fair for Blacks. By the 1960s, large numbers of Caribbean people were arriving. Today, there are no trades, professions, careers, or businesses from which Canadians can be excluded on the basis of their race, religion, or nationality.

New Canadians often appreciate the opportunities found in a free, democratic, multicultural country more than Canadians who were born here.

Politicians

In the Maritimes, early Black Loyalists frequently led, organized, and administered the Black communities. Abraham Shadd, in Ontario in 1859, and Mifflin Gibbs, in British Columbia in 1866, were politically active, but it would be 100 years before Blacks became established in politics.

In 1963, Leonard Braithwaite, a lawyer with a degree in business administration from Harvard University, became the first Black elected to a provincial parliament. He was a member of the Ontario Liberal Party. In 1968, Lincoln Alexander, a member of the Progressive Conservative Party, became the first Black elected to the House of Commons in Ottawa. He also became the first Black federal Cabinet minister. From 1985 to 1991, he was the first Black person to serve as lieutenant governor of Ontario. In 1972, in British Columbia, Rosemary Brown, who came to Canada in 1950 from Jamaica, was the first Black woman elected to a provincial parliament. In 1975, she ran for the leadership of the federal NDP party, but lost.

Dr. Monestime Saint Firmin became Canada's first Black mayor in Mattawa, Ontario, in 1974. In 1984, Daurene Lewis of Annapolis Royal, Nova Scotia, was the first Black woman elected mayor. She was a descendant of Rose Fortune. In 1984, Anne Cools, a social worker from Barbados, was made Canada's first Black senator. In 2005, Michaëlle Jean, a Haitian-born journalist and broadcaster working in Quebec, was appointed governor general of Canada.

Entertainers and Writers

Black Canadians have a long tradition in the entertainment business as musicians, singers, dancers, writers, and actors.

Oscar Peterson, born in Montreal in 1925, is Canada's most famous jazz musician. Toronto-born, singer-songwriter Dan Hill was the first Black

Canadian to achieve international recognition in pop music. Between 1977 and 1991, he produced 10 albums or CDs.

Maestro Fresh-Wes, born in Toronto in 1968, was the first major Canadian rap singer. His parents were from Guyana. In 1991, he won the first Juno Award for the best rap recording. In recent years, Black artists such as k-os, Rascalz, Saukrates, Choclair, and Kardinal have emerged.

Toronto-born Deborah Cox, a rhythm and blues artist, performed at the 1992 inauguration of President Bill Clinton in the U.S. She

Juno Award

volunteers with World Vision Canada, which helps poor children worldwide.

Nova Scotia-born, Black poet and playwright George Elliott Clarke, created the words for the opera "Beatrice Chancy," by James Rolfe. It depicts life in 1801 when slavery flourished at Annapolis Royal. It was first performed by Black opera soprano Measha Brueggergosman, who was born in Fredericton, New Brunswick. She also loves to perform Black spirituals.

Daniel G. Hill, born in the U.S., wrote *The Freedom Seekers: Blacks in Early Canada*. He became the first director of the Ontario Human Rights Commission and later Ombudsman of Ontario.

Born in Barbados, award-winning writer Austin Clarke came to Canada in 1955. He wrote a trilogy about Caribbean immigrants in Toronto. John Alleyne, also from Barbados, has won world recognition in ballet.

Dionne Brand came to Toronto from Trinidad at age 17. In 1997, she won the Governor General's Award for Poetry for *Land to Light On*. She also created *Earth Magic*, a book of poems for children. English-born, playwright

Djanet Sears moved to Saskatoon at age 15. In 1998, she received a Governor General's Award for Drama for *Harlem Duet*.

Lillian Allen, originally from Jamaica, won Juno Awards for dub poetry. Motion, a.k.a. Wendy Braithwaite, wrote *Motion in Poetry* and hosted a long-running radio show. She is one of many community activists. Rita Cox moved from Trinidad to Toronto to work as a librarian. Her unique, traditional story-telling captivates audiences around the world.

Order of Canada

Order of Canada

The Order of Canada is awarded for outstanding achievement. The first Black to receive one was Isaac Phills in 1967. He was a West Indian who moved to Cape Breton and became involved in his community. Since then, many Black citizens have received the honour, including Carrie Best, Nova Scotia's outspoken newspaper woman; Stanley Grizzle, a union organizer and the first Black federal citizenship judge; Donald Willard Moore, a Barbados-born, social activist; William Pearly Oliver, a Baptist minister and defender of equality; and Beverley Mascoll, a cosmetics entrepreneur who created beauty products specifically for Black women.

Black History Month

In 1995, Canada's government declared February as Black History Month.

Athletes

Black athletes have been participating in sports events and winning honours for themselves and Canada for many years.

Olympic Medal

Sprinter Harry Jermone, born in Prince Albert, Saskatchewan, won the bronze medal in the 1964 Tokyo Olympics in the 100-metre race. Ben Johnson came from Jamaica when he was 15 years old. At the Seoul Olympics in 1988, this sprinter became a Canadian hero when he won the gold medal in the men's 100-metre event. But his fame quickly turned to shame when it was taken away from him after he tested positive for illegal steroids. In 1990, North Vancouver runner Charmaine Crooks, born in Jamaica, became the first Canadian woman to run 800 metres in less than two minutes. Jamaican Donovan Bailey moved to Oakville, Ontario, with his family when he was 13. At the Atlanta Olympics in 1996, he captured the gold medal for the 100-metre race and set a world record of 9.84 seconds. With his teammates, Robert Esmie, Glenroy Gilbert, and Bruny Surin, Donovan won his second gold medal in the 100-metre relay. One of their coaches was Molly Killingbeck, a Black athlete who had won a silver medal for the 400-metre relay in the 1984 Olympic Games in Los Angeles.

Champion wrestler Daniel Igali of Burnaby, B.C., was born in Nigeria. He won the Olympic gold medal for Canada at the 2000 Olympics in Sydney, Australia. Boxer Lennox Lewis immigrated to Kitchener, Ontario, from London, England. In 1983, the teenager won the world junior boxing championship. In 1988, in Seoul, Korea, he became Canada's first Olympic boxing champion since 1932. In 1992, after turning professional, he took the

Ferguson Jenkins

World Boxing Championship and the British heavyweight title. He defeated Evander Holyfield, in 1999, to become Heavyweight Champion of the World. In 2002, he knocked out Mike Tyson in the eighth round to hold on to his title. He retired a champion in 2004.

Pitcher Ferguson Jenkins, a descendant of Underground Railroad fugitives, is from Chatham, Ontario. With the Boston Red Sox and Chicago Cubs, he won 284 games and struck out 3,192 batters. In 1991, he became the first Canadian elected to the Baseball Hall of Fame. The Toronto Blue Jays, with many Black players, won the World Series, back to back, in 1992 and 1993. Raptors basketball players also make Toronto their home.

In 1958, the first Black person to play in the National Hockey League was Willie O'Ree. Today, there are dozens of Black hockey stars. Goalie Grant Fuhr helped the Edmonton Oilers win five Stanley Cups between 1984 and 1990. Jarome Iginla, born in Edmonton, Alberta, scored two goals in the 2002 Winter Olympics to ensure a gold medal for Canada. Anson Carter, son of Barbados immigrants, scored an overtime goal to win gold for Canada at the world championships in May 2003.

Every five years, Statistics Canada takes a census of the number of people living in Canada. The last one before this book was published was in 2001. The next one will be in 2006.

If you go on the Internet to www.statcan.ca you will discover such statistics as the countries of origin of Black Canadians and the population in your province, or possibly your city. Statistics Canada shows you the numbers by ethnic origin and by visible minority.

Distribution of Blacks in Canada by provinces & territories (2001)	
Newfoundland	840
PEI	370
Nova Scotia	19,670
New Brunswick	3,850
Quebec	152,195
Ontario	411,095
Manitoba	12,820
Saskatchewan	4,165
Alberta	31,390
British Columbia	25,465
Yukon	115
Northwest Territories	170
Nunavut	65
Total in Canada	662,210

Canadian Black Heritage Crossword Puzzle

ACROSS:

1. When he came to Canada in 1858, John Brown planned a raid on the town of _____ Ferry.
7. Canada's first Black lawyer (1884).
9. In 1972, the first Black woman elected to a provincial parliament.
11. Escaped slave who became a newspaper editor.
12. An African storyteller.
15. A Black hockey player denied the chance to play in the NHL.
17. In the 1830s, at the Wilberforce settlement in Upper Canada, this former slave became known as Doc for his famous herbal medicines.
21. First Black female newspaper editor in N.A.
24. Some believe that he was "Uncle Tom."
25. He led his people back to Africa (Sierra Leone).
27. Henry Brown earned this nickname when he escaped slavery.
29. Canada's first policewoman.
30. He won a gold medal at the Olympics in 2000.
35. He received a V.C. for his bravery in 1857.
36. The first Black lieutenant governor of Ontario.
37. He participated in John Brown's raid in 1859.
38. The first known Black to live in Canada (1608).
40. Black community founded in 1850 at Chatham.
41. Elected Toronto alderman in 1894.
43. First successful all-Black settlement in New Brunswick (1812).
44. A town-crier in 1851 who was called the "walking newspaper."
45. Nova Scotia's largest Black community in 1784.
46. Jamaican rebel warriors who built the citadel in Halifax in 1796.

DOWN:

2. A Black teacher and doctor in the North-West Territories and Saskatchewan.
3. Famous Black inventor born in Ontario in 1844.
4. First elected Black mayor in Canada in Mattawa, Ontario (1974).
5. Early elected politician in Victoria in 1866.
6. A white man who created an all-Black community in Canada West in 1849.
8. Canada's first Black doctor (1857).
10. Famous NHL goalie for the Edmonton Oilers.
13. Soldier killed in Afghanistan in 2002.
14. A slave boy who arrived in Canada in 1628 and gained his freedom.
16. In an attempt to escape slavery in 1734, she burned down 46 houses in Montreal.
17. Leader of Nova Scotia's largest Black community in 1786.
18. First Black woman elected as a mayor (1984).
19. A white conductor on the URR from Belleville who made daring trips south to free slaves.
20. A famous Black cowboy from Alberta.
22. A World Champion boxer from Halifax (1891).
23. He abolished slavery in Upper Canada in 1793.
26. A famous female conductor on the URR.
28. Canada's most famous jazz musician.
31. A day of parades to celebrate freedom.
32. A famous Black school established in 1850.
33. The official granting of freedom to slaves.
34. She gained freedom, but it was taken away.
39. The continent that was the origin of slavery.
42. An escaped slave who caused a riot in Boston.

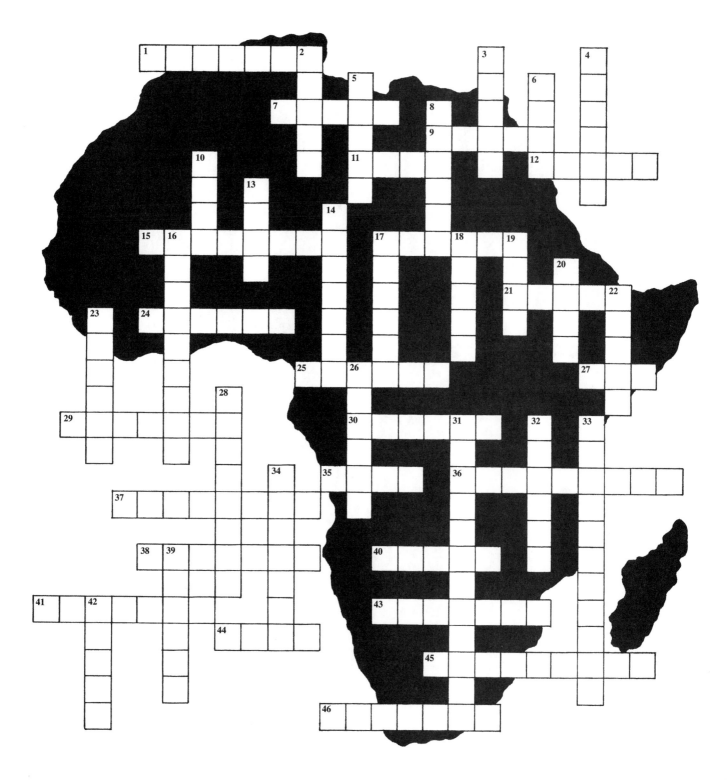

True Tails from the Dog Park

By Max and Luther

Illustrations by Julie Ann Stricklin

Visit our website: www.kariandcarey.com

Purchase our book:
www.maxandluther.com
www.amazon.com
www.barnesandnoble.com

First published by Dog Ear Publishing
4010 W. 86th Street, Ste H
Indianapolis, IN 46268
www.dogearpublishing.net

ISBN: 978-1-4575-3268-9

Library of Congress Control Number: has been applied for

This book is printed on acid-free paper.

Printed in the United States of America

Dedication:

This is for the 95% of our fellow dog friends whom we love and adore. The other 5% are the inspiration.

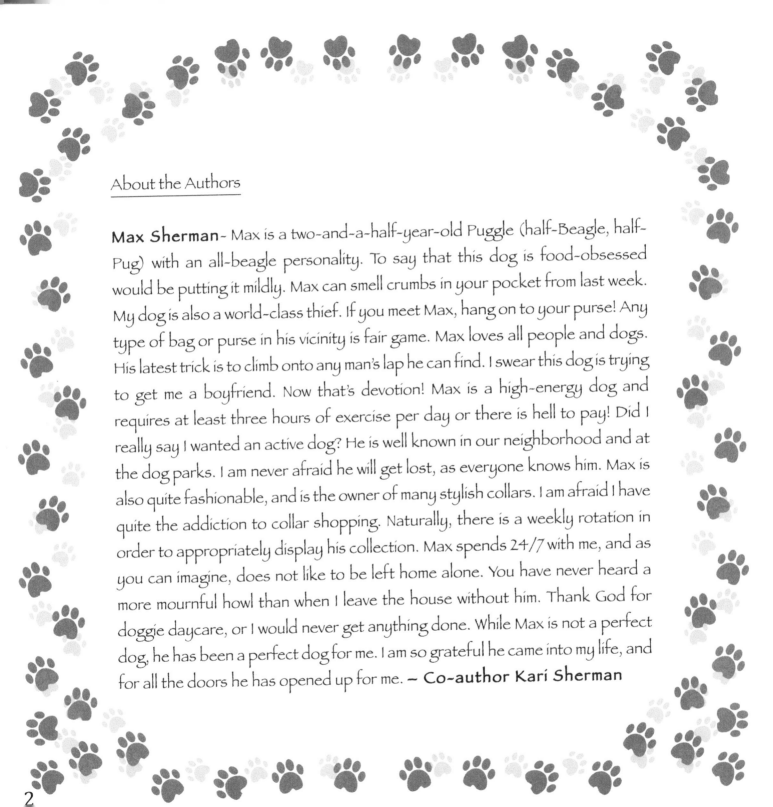

About the Authors

Max Sherman- Max is a two-and-a-half-year-old Puggle (half-Beagle, half-Pug) with an all-beagle personality. To say that this dog is food-obsessed would be putting it mildly. Max can smell crumbs in your pocket from last week. My dog is also a world-class thief. If you meet Max, hang on to your purse! Any type of bag or purse in his vicinity is fair game. Max loves all people and dogs. His latest trick is to climb onto any man's lap he can find. I swear this dog is trying to get me a boyfriend. Now that's devotion! Max is a high-energy dog and requires at least three hours of exercise per day or there is hell to pay! Did I really say I wanted an active dog? He is well known in our neighborhood and at the dog parks. I am never afraid he will get lost, as everyone knows him. Max is also quite fashionable, and is the owner of many stylish collars. I am afraid I have quite the addiction to collar shopping. Naturally, there is a weekly rotation in order to appropriately display his collection. Max spends 24/7 with me, and as you can imagine, does not like to be left home alone. You have never heard a more mournful howl than when I leave the house without him. Thank God for doggie daycare, or I would never get anything done. While Max is not a perfect dog, he has been a perfect dog for me. I am so grateful he came into my life, and for all the doors he has opened up for me. — **Co-author Kari Sherman**

Luther Laubenberg ("Lou") - Luther is a one-and-a-half-year-old Olde English Bulldog. Originally from Nunley Ranch in Pelham, Tennessee, he now resides in San Diego, California. Luther is a big lug. When you see him coming, it's best to get out of the way. He is like a freight train, slow to get going, and even slower to stop. He is also a big love. Luther is the sweetest and gentlest of souls. He loves everyone, except maybe his older Bulldog brother, Earl (especially when Earl is getting more attention than him). Luther loves all the little dogs and the puppies at the park. He will lie down, legs sprawled out behind him (we call it the "frog splash"), and let the little ones jump all over him, pull on his jowls, and nip at his bum. He never gets tired of it. Luther also has swagger. When he walks his stomach goes one direction, and his bum and head go the other way. People will stop to point and laugh. His swagger definitely gets people talking. Most people have never seen such a big and handsome Bulldog before. Luther loves the attention, and I love sharing him with others. At home, napping and cuddling are his favorite activities. When he is not hanging out on the couch, you will find him holding down the bed while snoring loudly—very loudly! ~ Co-author Carey Laubenberg

Dog Park Rules: Food Faux Paw

1. Do not bring treats to the dog park. You will be mobbed by every drooling dog.

2. Always ask the owner before offering any dog a treat due to allergies and weight issues.

3. Breakfast, lunch or dinner should be consumed at home and not at the dog park—it is not a human picnic area.

4. If you do bring food to a dog beach or a dog park, be aware that the dogs can and will steal your food. Getting angry at the dog owners is unfair and frankly, ridiculous.

5. Educate yourself on which foods are poisonous to dogs, such as chocolate, as this will save you money on expensive vet bills or unintended consequences.

Dog Beach Bandit

I am Max the Puggle, and I am food obsessed. (Hi, Max!) This means I will literally do anything and everything for food. I really enjoy stalking you the minute you approach with any food on your person, even leftover crumbs! At our local dog beach, I have developed quite a reputation for stealing food out of your bag, even if you are sitting right next to it. One time I ran half a mile down the beach as soon as I spotted a family on a beach blanket with a bag. A whole half a mile! I proceeded to reach in and grab a sandwich, still wrapped in a plastic bag, and I took off fast! I ate the sandwich, bag and all, in five seconds flat. My human can tell you it was no fun pulling the digested plastic bag from my bum three days later. We were yelled at and scolded by both the family and the lifeguard for this theft—seriously, it *is* a dog beach! **~ Max**

Dog Park Picnic

A woman and her children came into the dog park one day and set out a picnic lunch. They thought it would be fun to picnic there with their dogs. Well, the other dogs in the park thought that they had died and gone to heaven! Chaos and thievery ensued. The family scrambled to rescue their lunch from the pack while the other pet guardians attempted to restrain their own dogs. The mother looked up and said, "Perhaps I didn't think this idea through." The moral of this story is that even other pet parents can be clueless as to proper dog park behavior.
– Friends of Max and Luther

McDonald's

One day at the dog park, I saw a new guy enter the park with his two dogs. This man was wearing cool long shorts with pockets on the side. He reached down into his left side pocket and came up with a McDonald's Egg McMuffin! I naturally raced over to him to check it out. I had to jump on top of the picnic table in order to get to the savory treat. Some of my friends also came over to see if they could partake as well. It was party time! Unfortunately, the man did not feel like sharing this tasty morsel. All of us dogs were really sad. However, as soon as he finished his snack, the man reached down into his right side pocket and pulled out another muffin! We couldn't believe it! We barked and howled to no avail; the man ate that one as well. Whatever happened to the concept of sharing? My human was not amused, and shared her feelings with the man. We never saw him again. **– Max**

Another McDonald's Story

One of our friends at the dog park is a beautiful white husky named Spirit. Spirit is a foodie, like me. We are definitely kindred spirits! One day at the park, a man walked in with a white bag displaying a red and yellow arch on the side. Spirit could smell that bag from the far side of the park. He took off running towards the man as fast as he could go (which is really fast)! The man lifted the bag shoulder-high in anticipation of the dogs converging on his position, but what he did not count on was the fact that huskies can jump really high. Spirit grabbed the bag from the man in mid-air and landed five feet away. That was the last we saw of the tasty treat. Never underestimate a dog's jumping ability when it comes to food and toys! **– Friend of Max and Luther**

Dog Park Journal

Alert
Be on the lookout! Mak, a two-year old Bernese Mountain Dog, was caught on camera stealing a beach ball from a neighbor's yard. He is considered very playful. Mak has black, white and tan hair, a big head and a fluffy tail. Anyone who sees Mak, be cautious, do not approach as he may jump excessively. Please call your lo

ASK MAX

Feeding your dog scraps from the table encourages begging and weight issues. Best if you refrain.

Follow recommended proportions and frequency when feeding your dog; this will ensure a healthy weight and longer life for your best friend.

Dogs, unlike people, generally only eat when they are hungry.

Health Warning: Chinese treats
The FDA has issued a warning today regarding the beef jerky treats for dogs manufactured by China. Studies have shown that the treats may cause dogs to become violently ill. Local pet stores have removed product from their shelves. Check your pantry today and properly dispose of these items.

Summer Tips for Dogs
As summer fun begins, it is time to remind everyone of safe summer tips for dogs. Do not leave your dog in the car as you are running errands. Dogs easily dehydrate. They need access to shade and fresh clean water. Exercise your dog in the early morning or late evening when it is cooler!

Dog Park Rules: Poop Realities

1. We will step in it and then give you our paw to shake.

2. We will eat it and then give you a kiss. (Don't point it out to our humans; they are already aware of our habits).

3. Our humans will pick it up, but forever look at you with disdain.

4. Our humans will call it to your attention in front of everyone.

5. We will make sure your dog happens to roll in it before going home.

Picky Poop Eater

I am a poop eater. Not my poop, but other dogs' poop. It started when I was six months old. I think I was just curious at first. My human tried everything to stop this practice, but I am persistent. It's not all poop, or all the time. It just happens when the mood strikes. Apparently I am rather picky when it comes to this diet supplement, according to my human. I really keep her on her toes, because she has to maintain constant vigilance, which naturally is not aided by other dog guardians' inability to police their dog's poop. It's lucky for me, though! I have gotten better as I have aged, but I still feel the urge occasionally. Unfortunately, my human has been subjected to all kinds of comments from other dog parents, varying from sympathetic to rude. Not really helpful overall. It's best to keep your comments to yourself. No dog is perfect, neither are their guardians. ~ **Max**

Whoops!

I have this friend named Hesher, who is a 100+-pound gorgeous Bloodhound. We met at the dog park when we were both puppies. He was so much fun to play with! Hesher liked to run, play and roll in the grass. One day he rolled in the grass, not realizing that there was poop underneath him. He was such a mess and smelled really stinky. Boy was his mom mad! Bathing a large bloodhound like him was no easy task. After that incident, Hesher stopped coming to the dog park and I miss him! Please pick up after us dogs so we don't lose our favorite playmates. ~ **Max**

Dog Park Journal

Dog show coming to Fairgrounds

National Dog Show is coming to Del Mar December 1st. The show will be held at the fairgrounds from 9:00 A.M. until 4:00 P.M. Tickets will be $12 in advance, $15 at the door. Come see your favorite breeds compete for the national title of Best Dog!

Dog Park Donations

The Torrey Dog Park is in need of a water fountain and a few more trees for shade. During the summer months, the dogs are melting. Please send donations to the Torrey Dog Park Association.

Helpful Tips

Nothing is worse than when your dog has an upset stomach. There are certain foods that have been shown to be mild on their stomachs. These foods include but are not limited to the following: cottage cheese, scrambled eggs, and pumpkin. Always introduce a new dog food slowly as dogs are sensitive to

ASK LUTHER

🐾 Always pick up your dog's poop when walking your dog. The world and the sidewalk are not your backyard.

🐾 Always have extra poop bags on hand; you never know if you are going to need one.

🐾 There are many public areas that have free dog bags; take advantage of them.

🐾 At dog parks and beaches, it is your responsibility to pick up your dog's poop. Treat all places as if you live there. This will ensure a clean environment for all.

🐾 Knowing your dog's poop schedule will save you from unwanted accidents.

🐾 Picking up your dog's poop in a bag and then leaving the bag on the ground is not sufficient. Throw it in the garbage!

Grass at the Dog Park?

High School Dog Park needs new grass. If you are a regular at the dog park and are tired of getting dusty, or if you don't visit the park but agree the dogs deserve fresh grass, contact your local council member. Let them hear your opinion and hopefully we will be playing on fresh grass soon.

Notice

As summer approaches, so do the fleas. Remember to give your pet its flea medications on a regular basis. It is recommended to keep your dog on flea medications all year around, but it is especially important during the summer months. Protect your dog and yourself!

Traveling with your Dog?

Planning a trip to Del Mar, CA. and need a pet friendly hotel? Check out the Town of Del Mar website to find pet friendly hotels in the area. Discounts available.

Announcement

Happy Birthday Tip! It has been a great three years. You are the best dog.

Dog Park Rules: Dogs over Kids

1. Kids should be carefully monitored at the dog park. We don't know their age. We don't often realize we are bigger than they are. We just want to run and play with everyone, and we think everyone wants to run and play with us.

2. Kids can easily be knocked down, hurt or cause dogs to become irritated. If this is a problem for you, leave your kid at home.

3. Small children (in the arms of their parents) are frequently viewed by dogs as a fun toy! We will jump all over you to get at it!

4. Kid's toys are a terrible idea at the park. We will attempt to take them, as we do not know the difference between dog toys and kid toys. They all look the same.

5. Bikes, tricycles, skateboards, etc. are not a dog's best friend. Many of us are scared of them. Please do not bring them into the dog park.

6. Don't let your child name the new dog. You could end up with a dog named Sparkles and he is a boy!

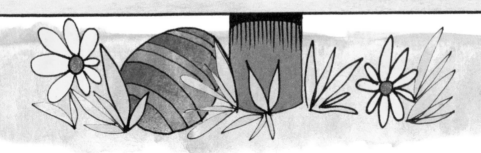

Endearing Emily

Boy, do I love babies! Most days, parents get nervous when they see me coming towards their little ones. They will lift them up to the sky, or they will turn their back to me, or even walk away. It makes me sad. I know I'm a big guy (105 pounds and still growing), but I'm gentle. Recently, however, a new baby appeared at the park. I sauntered over, thinking that the mom was going to start running in the opposite direction. To my surprise, not only did she not run, she held Emily out to meet me. Instant love! I was able to lick her little toes and her fingers. All the while, Emily was giggling in delight and petting my fur. My nub of a tail was going a mile a minute. We had so much fun! I even snuck in a kiss on her cheek. Emily's mom was terrific; she was giggling as well. Eventually they had to leave. I escorted them to the gate and tried to shove my big head through the fence for one last kiss. Emily waved good-bye, and her mom assured me that they would visit again. I'm so glad Emily's mom could see past my big, rough exterior. ~ **Luther**

Scooter Snafu

One day at the dog park, a mother and her two children came in with their dog, a bike and a scooter. The kids proceeded to ride their bikes up and down the dog park. Some of us dogs reacted poorly to this activity. My human suggested to the mother that perhaps the bike and the scooter were not a great idea in the dog park. She also pointed out that there was a playground next door. The mother did not take kindly to the suggestion, but did instruct her children to leave the dog park. Sometimes people do not take kindly to being shown the error of their ways. **-Max**

Tables and Chairs (Same family)

There is a picnic table in the dog park that people and dogs like to sit on. My favorite thing is to stand on top of the table to check things out and greet all the people. I even taught my pal Luther to climb up. It was quite a feat for him! He is big, but not agile. The same annoyed mother from the story above made a comment to my mom about us dogs being on top of the table. It was not in a nice tone of voice! My human replied that in the dog park we are allowed to pretty much do what we want. I guess the bicycle incident was not forgotten, nor forgiven. **~ Max**

Dog Park Playground

One day at the dog park, which is adjacent to a ballpark, a woman and her two kids came in and proceeded to put out a blanket. The family then emptied out a bag full of toys onto the blanket and started to play. Chaos ensued, as all of us canines came over to explore this newfound treasure trove. I grabbed some small plastic figurines and took off. My human chased me down and rescued the toys. She politely informed the mother that this perhaps wasn't the best idea at a dog park. Surprisingly, the mother was quite angry at us for interfering with their playtime. My owner again politely informed her that yes indeed; this was a dog park and not a playground. She was concerned for the welfare of the dogs, as small plastic toys could easily be swallowed. It is interesting that we (dogs) are unwelcome at playgrounds for children, but not the other way around. ~ **Max and Luther**

15

Dog Park Journal

Rescue Organization

Want a new dog? Have you considered adoption? You can find puppies, senior dogs, big dogs, small dogs, skinny dogs, and chubby dogs. You can find playful dogs, quiet dogs, working dogs, or dogs that like to snuggle. Contact your local pet rescue organization for further information.

Vaccines

Vaccines are an important part of your dog's continuing health. Add reminders to your calendar for the various vaccines needed: rabies, fecal analysis, bordetella, parvo and DHP3. Remember some daycares required updated vaccines every six months versus a year. Schedule your vet appointment today!

Announcement

Congratulations to Greta the English Mastiff for winning Best in Breed. Her blocky head, large yet perfect proportions and amazing personality put her at the top of her class. Way to go Greta!

ASK MAX

Teaching children proper dog greeting and petting etiquette will prevent many incidents.

Children should be taught not to be afraid of any animals.

Know your child's reaction to all size dogs prior to coming to the dog park, as screaming children freak us out.

Dog Classes

There are a variety of classes available these days for you and your dog which are beyond the basic training classes. One of the classes that has been gaining in popularity is agility classes. Your dog learns to run a complicated course and you get some exercise too! Explore the classes available in your area.

Dog Therapy Work

Want to give back to your community? Have you considered Pet Therapy work? You and your owner can visit hospitals, senior centers, schools, really anywhere you think a pet will bring a smile. If this sounds interesting, contact your local pet therapy organization for more details.

Advertisement

Tired of the same old collar? Is it dirty and smelly? Time for a new custom made collar by Shermie Design. These collars are not only unique but are machine washable. Call today for more info! 555-0101.

Dog Park Rules: Practices for People

1. Just because you have a dog, it does not make you an expert on all dogs.

2. Wearing nice clothes at a dog park is not the best idea unless you don't care about the dirt.

3. The more in the wrong you are, the louder you will argue your case.

4. Don't worry about not knowing someone's name if you know us (dogs), you are good. Chances are our owners forgot your name, too!

5. Our guardians are responsible and liable for our actions.

6. If you are worried for your safety (getting knocked over), realize it might happen. Be prepared, and enter at your own risk.

7. If you decide to sit or even lay on the ground at the dog park, don't be shocked when you are trampled or even peed on. We are dogs, and this our dog park!

Tennis, Anyone?

A woman wearing a sparkling white tennis outfit walked into the dog park with her Golden Retriever puppy. The puppy was sweet and loving, and proceeded to kiss and jump on all the people there (it was a Retriever, after all!). I was a puppy at the time as well, and decided to return the favor. I jumped on the woman and gave her a big kiss. The woman shrieked in horror, and desperately wiped off her immaculate outfit. My human naturally corralled me and apologized to her. She sternly told my mom that I am not well behaved and should be banned from the park. My guardian laughed hysterically, and pointed out to her that *her* dog was all over everyone else. She quickly left in a huff. The moral of the story is to leave your nice clothes at home, and bring your sense of humor! ~ **Max**

Russian Roulette

People and dogs come and go at the dog park. There are the regulars who are there every day at the same time come rain or shine, and then there are the newbies. One such newbie to the dog park was a nice but loud European woman. She and her new puppy had been coming to the dog park for about a week. The woman was still learning how to discipline and take care of her very active dog. One day she came in with a squirt bottle, as her dog tended to jump on people. I had taken a liking to a cute Lab and was intent on humping the poor guy. My human, of course, was policing the situation; unfortunately, she did get distracted for a couple of seconds. When she turned around, the loud woman was squirting me in the face! Can you believe it?! As my guardian inquired what the hell she was doing, Loud Woman replied that I was humping the other dog. Mom informed her in no uncertain terms that one should NEVER discipline someone else's dog. She apologized and walked away. Not ten minutes later she was squirting someone else's dog! I have to say, she did have good aim. - **Max**

Open House

There is a section of my local dog beach that is bordered by multi-million dollar houses. These houses are so big and pretty, with direct access down to the beach. How I wish that my mom owned one of these places! One day I was playing on the beach in front of one of these houses with some of the other dogs. One of these dogs, who actually lived in the beautiful beach house, decided it was time to go home. His owners conveniently left the gate to the stairs open. Well, I was not done playing with this dog, so I followed him up the stairs to the house. My mom started yelling for me, but I ignored her. It was a great patio to play in, with lots of people hanging out. My mom followed me up the stairs but I was too quick for her. I jumped the stone wall separating this house from the one next door. There were lots of people on this patio, too! All the people at both houses got really quiet and started to stare at my mom, who was still chasing me. Mom did not look very happy with me, and the people at the houses did not look very happy with her, either. Well, I decided that I'd had enough fun, so I sat down and waited for Mom to catch up with me. Needless to say, our day at the beach was over. I thought that people who owned big houses on a dog beach would be more sympathetic to my mom, but not all people who have dogs are as nice as my mom. ~ **Max**

Allergic to the Beach

It was a typical day at the dog beach. My human and I were having fun running around and meeting new people. I spotted a couple sitting on the rocks, enjoying their coffee and muffins. Well, did I mention they had muffins? Off I went, to greet the new people and perhaps steal some food. My mom quickly followed in damage-control mode. I circled the couple a few times. My mom laughed and apologized while explaining that I have a severe food obsession. The man was visibly upset, and asked my human to please remove me from the beach. He was allergic! Yes, allergic to dogs! My mom and I were stunned at this revelation. When she recovered from the shock, she replied, "You do realize you are at a dog beach, right?" He quickly responded, "Well, people can come here, too!" It just goes to show you that sometimes people are not as smart as some dogs. - **Max**

Pee Perfect

Three of our friends were at their dog park in Arizona when a man sauntered in. He proceeded to lie down in the grass. Yes, the grass, where we all pee. So one of my friends saw this new object in the middle of the park and went over to mark his territory. Translation: He peed on the man. The man became irate. He began to yell, swear and threaten my friends and their guardian. What did he think was going to happen? He laid on the ground at a dog park! Not too bright.
- Friends of Luther and Max

Dog Park Journal

New Housing Amenities

Recently builders are offering new add-on options for your house. One of these options is a pet washing station in your laundry room. This is just another example of how our dogs are an integral part of our families. Ask your builder today about this option.

Luther's Birthday Announcement

Come one; come all to Luther's birthday bash. It will be held Saturday December 31st at the dog park. We will have coffee, hot cocoa, cookies, muffins, and treats galore. Don't miss the fun and a chance to bring in the New Year with all your closest dog park friends!

Advertisement

Your local pet store is offering puppy classes I and II for a low, low price of $120 per course. Class I focuses on the seven basic commands: sit, down, come, stay, off, no and drop. Class II focuses on leash training. Call today to sign up for your group session.

ASK LUTHER

If you think your dog can do no wrong, and feel the need to reprimand everyone else's dog, please refrain from doing so. It is the dog park. Relax. And if you still can't let it go, speak to our humans; they will set you straight.

Understand your dog's play versus fear reactions. Sometimes it isn't "just playing." If you see your dog chasing another dog and the owner is screaming for help, chances are they are not having fun. Go help out!

Always be aware of your surroundings. Dogs will easily knock you off your feet if you are not paying attention.

The dog park is not day care. You need to pay attention to your dog, not the phone!

If you are allergic to dogs, then the dog park or dog beach is clearly not for you.

Lost Dog Alert

Daisy, a Labrador retriever, was reported missing near dog beach in Del Mar, CA. Daisy was last seen running down the Coast Highway. Please call 555-8000 to report any sightings. Remember to micro-chip your dog!

Max and Luther are coming!

Max and Luther will be at the Del Mar Pet Store on Saturday December 1st from 12-1. They will be signing copies of their new book "True Tails from the Dog Park". Be the first to get a copy. Don't miss out.

Dog Behaving Badly?

Are you having trouble with chewing, barking, biting, not playing well with others? Are you getting ejected from the dog park, owners refusing to take you out in public? Maybe it's time you saw a behaviorist. They will help you get to the root of your issues and set up a plan so that you can lead a normal and productive life.

Dog Park Rules: Toy Truths

1. If your dog (or child) has a special toy and they will be heartbroken without it, don't bring it to the dog park. It will become everyone's favorite toy, and will never be seen (in one piece) again.

2. If your dog is aggressive, even if just with its own toys, the dog park is not the place for you.

3. All items such as keys, bags, hats, etc. lying around at the dog park are fair game. If something is valuable, the dog park is not the place for it.

4. Small toys are easily swallowed by large dogs. Be aware of such items in a mixed-size dog park.

5. Some dogs' favorite toys are free. Fetch that stick, my friend! Chew that water bottle!!!

6. There is no such thing as an indestructible toy.

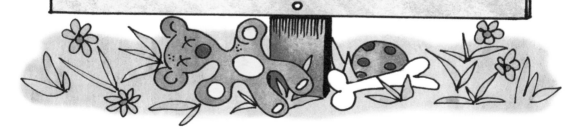

Winston's Frisbee

Winston and his mom are regulars at the dog park. Winston is a Bulldog on a mission. He comes bearing his favorite Frisbee toy in his mouth. Winston does not move very fast, so his owner only throws the Frisbee a few feet at a time. It is always fun to watch him play fetch. One problem with Winston is that he does not like to share his toy with the other dogs. I am not a fan of the game of fetch; however, I do enjoy the Frisbee occasionally, and Winston's Frisbee is my favorite! Every time they come to the park, it is a race to the Frisbee. I am sure it is quite funny to watch— Puggle versus Bulldog. Guess who wins? Unfortunately, his human doesn't always think so. She gets quite annoyed with my quick and thieving ways. Chasing me down and removing said Frisbee becomes a fun game as well. Remember; if your dog has a favorite toy at the park, other dogs will like it too. ~ **Max**

Chess, Anyone?

One day at the dog park, a couple walked in with their dogs and a board game. They set up their game and proceeded to play. The game looked like fun. So many pieces to chew! So I ambled over. First I tried to reach my face up to the table. I could just make it, and I proceeded to knock over a piece or two. Surprisingly, they kept playing. My second attempt was more effective. I climbed onto the table and I placed myself right in the center of the game. Chess pieces went flying. Can you say bull in a china shop?! Game over. Mission accomplished. ~ **Luther**

Dog Park Journal

Dog Rescue Story

Brady a beautiful Golden Retriever was originally purchased from a breeder when he was eight weeks old. His owner proceeded to kennel this puppy until he was seven months old. Next, the owner decided to send him away for training. The poor puppy was afraid of its own shadow and had no socialization with other dogs at all. After training was completed, the owner decided he did not want Brady. Lucky for Brady, a new family moved in down the street who were ready to welcome a dog into their home. Within two months, Brady was a different dog. Happy, playful and full of life! What a difference a happy household can make.

Alert

Missing favorite toy: Pink stuffed elephant beloved by Jenny, the pit bull mix. If found, please contact us at 867-5309. Jenny misses her toy!

ASK MAX

Trying to retrieve your dog's toy from another dog is frustrating and nearly impossible. Discuss with the pet parent as to how to get it back, and consider leaving it at home next time if it bothers you.

Unwanted or unused dog toys you have at home could be a fun toy for us. Bring them to the dog park and share!

Take advantage of sales of dog toys. Purchase multiples and share one with your dog park friends.

Marshalls and Target have good, cheap dog toys.

Pet Friendly Places in San Diego

Del Mar is one of the towns in San Diego County which is very pet friendly. The town boasts a dog beach, multiple dog parks and restaurants that welcome dogs. If you are looking for a place to visit with Fido, think Del Mar, California.

Alert

Coyotes have been spotted in Crest Canyon. Keep your dogs leased and be on the look-out.

Dog Park Donations

Balboa Dog Park is looking for donations for the installation of lights. This highly visited dog park needs night-time lighting for the dark winter months. Working parents have a hard time finding a place to exercise their dogs after work. Lights at the park could be the answer. Interested in becoming a corporate sponsor? Call the Balboa Park Society today.

Dog Park Rules: Grooming Tidbits

1. Understand the grooming needs of your dog. Every dog has different needs.

2. Clothes do not make the dog. Dogs are not people. Less is more here.

3. We come with dirt, slobber and other less than sanitary conditions. Get used to it.

4. It is important to pay attention to our ears, nose and paws, as they are less obvious spots in regards to keeping us clean and infection free.

5. We require regular dental hygiene. When we kiss you, you will want us to have fresh dog breath!

Buford

In our neighborhood lives a beautiful Saint Bernard named Buford. He was one of the first dogs I met. He would lay stretched out on the ground and let me climb all over him and play. I had so much fun crawling all over this big guy. As most people know, Saint Bernard's are one of the most prolific droolers in the animal kingdom. In order to combat this, Buford's owner carried a clean rag in his pocket wherever they went. I thought this was one of the most clever and considerate ideas I had ever seen. Just in case other owners are not so on the ball, remember that certain breeds can and will drool on you. Beware! — **Max**

Glowing Golden

The sight of a Golden Retriever post-grooming appointment is a sight to behold: golden fur flowing in the wind, perfectly combed. Irresistible! Especially to those of us who have short hair and will never experience wind flowing through our fur. So, one day I spotted such a dog entering the park; head held high, fur flowing, and prancing like they owned the place. I couldn't resist. I sidled on over, using my swagger to distract them from the fact that I had a long "shoestring" of drool hanging from my jowls, and I wiped my face right across their back. I wanted to feel what it was like to have golden locks. The owner screamed in horror. Her poor dog had just been groomed, and now he was "filthy." Filthy? I don't think so. It's just a little drool. How can you say a little spit ruined a blow dry? A little wipe of a towel and it's like new. At least that's what my human tried to convince the Retriever's mom. She wasn't buying it; in fact, she was angry. She was angry enough to suggest that we move to another part of the park or better yet, leave. My mom suggested that if the grooming was that important, maybe she should have taken her dog for a walk instead. If it had not been the drool that ruined her dog, it probably would have been dog park dirt. Maybe she should relax and let her dog have a little fun. A dirty dog is a happy dog. ~ **Luther**

Dog Park Journal

ASK LUTHER

Cardiff Dog Days of Summer

This festival starts Saturday August 9, 2014 from 10am to 5pm. Activities include: Tibetan Blessing of the dog, ugly dog contest, vendor booths, games and so much more. If you are looking for some fun activities for you and your four legged friend, join us this Saturday. Admission is free.

Advertisement

Gear up for game day! Dog outfits with your team logo are now available on our website. Free Shipping if you purchase by August 30th. www.NFLdoggear.com.

Do Dogs get Jealous?

A new study conducted by University of California, San Diego explored dog behaviors associated with jealousy. It is no surprise to dog owners that dogs do indeed exhibit jealous behaviors. The study suggests not only that dogs do engage in what appear to be jealous behaviors but that they

Set a regular grooming schedule for your dog that includes bath, nails, and teeth. It is easier to keep up a set routine.

Most grooming items can be done at home, but there are plenty of services out there to be taken advantage of.

Begin teeth brushing early in your dog's life. They will get used to it, and the preventive benefits are huge ($$).

If your dog was just groomed and you want it to last more than a few hours, skip the beach or dog park, as they will get dirty. Go for a walk instead.

A dirty dog is likely to be a tired and happy dog.

Does your dog understand you?

A report published by Current Biology indicates that dogs not only pick up on the words we say, but also on our intent to communicate with them. This study could help to explain why we treat our dogs like we would treat our children. The researcher indicated that dog's reception to human communication is similar to that of your children. Remember dogs are sensitive to our tone. Be kind!

Dog Crates, Kennels and Carriers

Visit your local pet store today to see our latest line of dog crates, kennels and carriers. We have all sizes from small to extra-large. Mats are included! Sorry no pet strollers. They are too humiliating. Come in today and ask about our special discounts.

Dog Park Rules: Health and Happiness

1. Take note of any changes in our normal behavior. Remember, we cannot tell you what is wrong or what hurts.

2. If your dog is not neutered/spayed, and you come to the dog park, don't be surprised when everyone wants to be your dog's new "best friend." Be responsible and spay/neuter.

3. Remember that regular vet visits and vaccines will keep us, and subsequently other dogs, healthy.

4. Make sure that your dog always has access to clean, fresh water, especially in the summer. We dehydrate easily.

5. We are routine oriented. Changes in our routine can cause stress

Beware of the Beagles

As in everywhere one may go, there are those unique individuals who draw notice. At our local dog park, there is a woman with two Beagles who comes to the park daily. This woman not only talks to her dogs, but also to herself. It is sometimes hard to figure out who she is actually addressing. Her two Beagles are very vocal, as Beagles tend to be, and you can hear them coming from a mile away. The Beagles are what we like to call "senior" dogs. One Beagle always has a cast on its leg, although I am still unsure as to why. The other beagle has some back issues. Every time she enters the dog park, I get excited and trot over to her and her dogs. I love greeting all the newcomers. Every time she freaks out because of her dogs' health issues. She starts screaming before I even reach her, which frightens me. My human always comes over to steer me in another direction. The lady continues to reprimand me for getting in the vicinity of her dogs, and she then proceeds to have a long conversation with her dogs about unruly puppies and their owners. I don't understand why she brings her dogs to the park if they can't interact with any of us. If your pet has special needs, please reconsider bringing them to the dog park. It would be better for everyone. — **Luther**

Two ACL Lou

Hi, all. Let me start by saying, "I LOVE to play at the dog park." I call my style of play: **Splatter, Smother and Cover**. First, I brazenly side-swipe my opponent, knocking them to the ground. Next, I stand over them, assuring they can't escape. Then I flop on top of them, pinning them to the ground. It's hilarious watching them flail about. Unfortunately, this rough-housing led to not one but *two* ruptured ACLs. While I was recovering, my human figured out a way to get me to the park to see my pals without risking my recovery. First we visited from the opposite side of the fence. I was able to see everyone without the fear of being pounced upon. Once I was further along in my recovery, we visited the park during quiet times. This way I could meander around off-leash. As soon as the park became busy, we would head home. This was a great plan. My recovery went smoothly, and I was still able to be at the park with my pals. A happy Lou means a happy guardian! **~ Luther**

Inspirational

There is a great dog walker who comes to the dog park every day with between eight and ten dogs. She is so fantastic, and always has treats for me! One day she came with a new puppy that only had three legs. The dog was only six months old when he was hit by a FedEx truck and lost his leg. Well, you would never know that he was disabled by the way he played with me. He wrestled and ran around the park like every other puppy we know. I really liked him. He had such a sweet and playful personality. The dog walker told my mom that his family could not afford to keep him with all his problems, but that they had found him a new family. This new family raised funds to fit him with a new prosthetic limb. The puppy no longer comes to the dog park, but we heard that he was doing great. It is amazing how resilient we dogs are and how great our pet parents can be! ~ **Friend of Max and Luther**

True Love

My mom told me a story about a time before she had me, and before she understood how much dogs are loved by their guardians. She knew a man from work who had two great dogs, and one day one of his dogs got really sick. The vet had no conventional treatment for his illness, but suggested an experimental procedure that was both risky and costly, with no guarantee that it would work. The man decided to try the procedure because he wasn't ready to let his dog go. After two weeks and thousands of dollars later, the dog pulled through and got better. The man devoted so much of his time and energy to save his dog. My mom said she never really understood his devotion until she had me. How one's perspective changes! ~ **Max**

Dog Park Journal

Sports News

Tug-O-War Finals. Results are in! The Del Mar Dobermans beat the South Bay Spaniels 4-3 in a triple overtime grudge match. Congrats to the Dobermans for their third consecutive win!

Exercise Classes

Are you looking to get in shape? Stay in shape? Train for a competition? Train for life? FS Training can help you reach your goals. FS Training provides long walks, short sprints, agility courses, and nutrition advice. The time is now. Call FS Training at 888-444-8888.

Advertisement

For Sale-Hardly used XL black leather double spiked collar. It was worn only once for a Halloween party. I dressed as a Marine Mascot. If interested, call Earl for details.

ASK MAX

Knowing the typical health issues of your chosen breed will allow you to watch for any warning signs.

❧

Benadryl can be a dog owner's best friend. It will make us sleepy and calm. A calm dog makes for a happy owner.

❧

Pumpkin can help keep our digestive tract healthy (no diarrhea)! Yeah!!!

❧

Cottage cheese, sticky white rice and scrambled eggs are also good for upset stomachs.

❧

The color and consistency of your dog's poop is a good health indicator. It helps to pay attention.

Vets R Us

Are you suffering from a sore back, aching feet, or tight muscles? Maybe it is time to see your local veterinarian. There is no need to live with the discomfort when your vet will have the solution. One office visit is all you need to be put on the road to recovery. Call your Veterinarian now and start enjoying your day.

Dental Care

Dental Care Awareness Month Is February - Schedule your teeth cleaning in February and receive 2 free tubes of liver flavored toothpaste. What a great way to prepare for Valentine's Day- a clean mouth!

Dog Beach Petition

Unleashed dogs are prohibited on Dog Beach during the summer months. We believe this to be unacceptable. There are numerous beaches for vacationers to visit, why do they need Dog Beach as well? Please help us regain Dog Beach during the summer and sign our local petition.

Dog Park Rules: Neighborly Behavior

1. It is important to know how your dog behaves on and off-leash towards other dogs.

2. Understand your dog's play behavior and alarm triggers.

3. Do not assume that a dog will behave as the breed standard indicates; all dogs are a product of their upbringing.

4. Just because your dog is trained to walk off-leash does not mean that it is a good idea to do it.

5. Always ask the owner before approaching a strange dog. They will let you know if it's okay.

Little White Dog Wrangling

One day at the dog park, the following situation occurred. There was a handsome black Pit bull playing with its human when a small white dog entered the park. The little dog was extremely yappy, and liked to get in other dogs' faces. When the white dog started barking in the Pit bull's face, the Pit bull snatched up the white dog and vigorously shook the little thing. The owner quickly broke up the fight, but not before the little dog was seriously injured. I have never heard a more distressed howl of pain from a creature before. Luckily there was a vet close by, and the dog was treated for its injuries. The white dog was newly rescued from the animal shelter, and the guardian was not aware of its behavior issues/patterns. It was extremely unfortunate all around. We never did find out if the Pittie owner followed up with the other dog owner as to costs and liability. It is so important to know your dog and pay attention to what is going on at the park. We hate seeing these situations occur. **~ Max and Luther**

Ollie's Escape

Ollie and I are great friends. We met when I was a puppy and Ollie was newly rescued. Ollie and I spend a lot of time together, and Ollie is a frequent guest at our house. Ollie and his human, Andrea, live a block away across a busy street. One day, Andrea went to the grocery store down the street with Ollie. As usual she tied him up outside of the store while she shopped. Halfway through the store, she heard over the intercom that there was a little white dog on the loose in the parking lot. Shoot! That had to be her dog Ollie! She dropped her groceries and raced out the door, followed closely by the Starbucks guy and the bag boy. Sure enough, there was her dog, racing around the parking lot being chased by some Good Samaritans. Suddenly Ollie took off out of the parking lot and disappeared down the road. All the people were worried that the dog would run out into the street and get hurt, but not Andrea. The minute he left the parking lot she knew where he was headed. I just happen to live next door to the grocery store and sure enough, as she approached my house, there was her dog Ollie. He was patiently waiting for me to get home! Of course, the Starbucks guy and the bag boy who followed her could not believe that the dog was just calmly sitting at the door. Dogs are so smart! **– Max**

Dog Park Journal

Take Your Dog to Work Day
June 20th is take your dog to work day. Studies have shown that dogs alleviate stress and promote better moods. Tips for bringing your dog to work include: only bring well-trained dogs, puppy-proof your office, notify your co-workers and ensure that your dog has access to food, water, and especially toys!

Health Alert
Dairy can cause both diarrhea and vomiting in dogs. The culprit is the lactose in dairy products. A little diary can be fine but be aware of your dog's reaction to this delicious treat.

Biking with your Dog
Biking with your dog can be an enjoyable experience. This activity is especially great for high energy dogs where a walk is just foreplay. Consider your dog's age. Strenuous exercise is not recommended for dogs until they reach their maturity (between 18 months and 2 years depending on the breed).

ASK LUTHER

Always let a dog come to you and offer your hand for them to sniff.

Most dogs do not like to be petted on the top of the head; under the chin is better. Behind the ears is great, too!

Not all so-called aggressive breeds (Pit bulls, Rottweiler, etc.) are aggressive. Judge each dog on its own merits. Early socialization pays great dividends.

When purchasing/rescuing a dog, do your homework. Look out for potential red flags.

Be clear on what type of dog and personality you are looking for. Understand your lifestyle, economic, and time commitment requirements.

Be prepared by arming yourself with as much information as possible. Check out the questionnaire on Petfinder.com.

Pool Safety Tips
It is important to familiarize your dog with the pool prior to letting him just jump in. Teach your dog where the exits (steps) are. Test your dog's ability to get out of the pool from all angles. Never leave your dog unattended by the pool. Accidents can happen. Pool gates are readily available. Consider a life jacket for your pooch. Enjoy the summer!

Summer Treats for Dogs
Create your own frozen treats for your furry friend. Mix cottage cheese, water and something savory like peanut butter and freeze. Yum! Other ideas include mixing pumpkin, yogurt, and water or leftover hamburger, cheese and water. Your dog will love these frozen treats!

Help Wanted
Looking for a dog walker/runner for a special family member. Would be needed Monday through Friday for an hour mid-day. Will pay top dollar. References are required. Contact Steph at 555-6000.

Dog Park Rules: Good Citizenship Award

1. If you are standing near the water fountain and a bunch of panting dogs are staring at you, please turn on the fountain. Our owners would do the same for your dog.

2. If you have an issue with us on benches or picnic tables at the dog park, get over it. This is the one place we can let loose and have fun.

3. Always use the appropriate dog gates at the park. They ensure that the other dogs won't escape. We will try to make a break for it!

4. If you plan on reading a book, checking your e-mail, etc. while at the park, we would appreciate it if you paid more attention to your dog. What if your dog poops, is getting attacked by another dog, or is doing the attacking? You need to be aware. It is not the other dog owners' responsibility to look after your dog.

5. If you get drooled on, don't scream as if you have just contracted a fatal disease. It's only drool; you are at a dog park, and you will live!

Macho Min Pin

At our park there is a Miniature Pinscher who is not neutered. He is very assertive. He LOVES everybody. Big, small, furry or not, he does not discriminate. At first, I thought it was pretty funny. He would latch onto someone and hold on for dear life. It was all fun and games until he noticed me. He would not leave me alone. I'm a big guy, and I couldn't shake him! People were pointing and laughing. His guardian didn't seem to notice or care. How could he not notice? The situation became unbearable. Finally my human pointed out the situation to his owner. He acted like it wasn't a big deal and begrudgingly pulled the little guy off me. Thank goodness. Freedom! **– Luther**

Pampered Pomeranian

I love playing with other dogs, big or small. One day, a new Pomeranian puppy and her mom showed up at the park. The Pom was so cute, small and fluffy. I couldn't wait to go play with her, so I raced over and started wrestling with her. Well, her guardian was unsettled, to say the least. My mom likes to call these kinds of owners "helicopter" parents. They like to hover, and are unsure if their dogs should really play with other dogs. My mom assured her that I was very friendly and was just playing. After a few minutes, the other mom couldn't take it anymore and picked up her dog. Well, that was just an invitation to jump up on her and try to get to the puppy. Over the next month or so, my new friend kept coming to the park to play, and play we did. Unfortunately, every time the guardian would eventually pick up the puppy and leave in a huff. I never could understand it; we were having fun! Eventually they stopped coming to the park. I was sad. I'll never understand those helicopter parents; if they don't want their dogs to play with me, why do they come to the park? **– Max**

Mistaken Identity

One day, Luna's mom heard some rustling outside. She found a yellow Lab puppy in her front yard, hanging out and having fun. The Lab did not have any tags or identification on him. Luna's mom thought he might be Buddy, the yellow lab who lives behind them. She put a leash on "Buddy" and walked toward his house. He seemed to know exactly where he was going, and walked right up to the house. No one was home, so Luna's mom put him in the backyard to make sure he was safe. Job well done, she thought! A few hours later she heard people yelling for Tucker. She went outside and inquired as to whom they were searching for—a yellow Lab! Oops. Luna's mom mentioned to them that she knew where he was. The group went to "Buddy's" house and retrieved Tucker. Thankfully, no one was home yet. Tucker's owner was very upset. How could Luna's mom throw him in a stranger's backyard? Would she have preferred her to do nothing? Luna's mom pointed out that he had no identification. The owner showed her his collar with the tags. Luna's mom again pointed out that it was not on the dog at the time! The owner grabbed her dog in a huff and stormed off. No thanks, no appreciation that her dog was safe, nothing. Dog parents should look out for one another and their pets. No one wants to have their dog roaming the streets, hungry...or worse. — **Told to Max and Luther by Luna**

Dog Park Journal

Hero Dog!
Ani the 5 -year old Newfoundland saves a young boy from drowning. Lifeguards noticed a young boy being dragged out to sea by the tide. They were unable to reach him because of the strength of the current, so they sent Ani to get the job done. Her strength and determination allowed her to reach the boy and pull him to safety. Other than being a little scared and cold, the young boy was fine thanks to her quick action. She is a hero!

Most Popular Dog Games
1. Fetch
2. Hide-n-Seek
3. Find the Treat
4. Tug of War
5. Swimming
6. Hoops, Frisbee, Soccer

Obituary
RIP Sydney Vicious-Dear Syd, you left us way too soon. We miss your sweet face and your bossy personality. Who is going to guide us through life? We hope you are watching over us. We promise to behave -Earl and Luther.

ASK MAX

🐾 As a pet guardian, pass along your knowledge of dogs and etiquette to new dog parents. It will help them be a better, more confident guardian, and that will help their dogs to be confident as well.

🐾 Teach us basic commands: sit, stay, down, off, four on the floor. Other pet parents will be thankful and impressed.

🐾 Refrain from commenting on another dog parent's style of discipline. As with children, unless there is obvious abuse, it is better to keep your opinions to yourself.

🐾 Be courteous and be smart-knowledge and manners go a long way.

Sports News
Tug-O-War Finals. Results are in! The Del Mar Dobermans beat the South Bay Spaniels 4-3 in a triple overtime grudge match. Congrats to the Dobermans for their third consecutive win!

Exercise Classes
Are you looking to get in shape? Stay in shape? Train for a competition? Train for life? FS Training can help you reach your goals. FS Training provides long walks, short sprints, agility courses, and nutrition advice. The time is now. Call FS Training at 888-444-8888.

Advertisement
For Sale-Hardly used XL black leather double spiked collar. It was worn only once for a Halloween party. I dressed as a Marine Mascot. If interested, call Earl for details.

Chapter X – Earl's Corner

Hi, my name is Earl (Luther's older, wiser Bulldog brother), and I have a thing or two to say. First, when hanging out at the dog park, be aware of your surroundings. We are dogs, and we aren't always aware of our surroundings. We may step on your toes, drool on your clothes, or we may even run into you. When I see my Aunt Kari I run to greet her. If you think my brother is a freight train, I'm an extra-large (and wide) freight train! If you get in the way, I will take you down. Not intentionally, but I can't stop on a dime, nor am I agile enough to dodge out of the way. Be on the look-out for me or any rambling dogs while you are at the park. It will definitely save you from a trip to the hospital.

Secondly, know your dog. There is nothing worse than an oblivious dog owner, or an owner who thinks their dog can do no wrong. I can't express to you enough how annoying this can be. One day I joined my brother Luther and my guardian at the park. It was a nice, relaxing afternoon, until...a crazy Doodle arrived. Yes, I said it—crazy Doodle! This guy was all over everyone, dog and human alike. At first it was sort of funny. He was so happy to be running wild. But after 10 minutes I grew cranky. I did not come to the park to be used as a trampoline. My guardian realized my dismay and tried to shoo the Doodle away. He was not deterred. So we decided to leave the park early because my nerves were shot. Yes, we had to leave! And where was his owner? On the phone! He was oblivious to the fact that his dog was annoying almost everyone. If only his owner had taken control of his crazy Doodle, maybe we all could have enjoyed a full afternoon at the park.

Lastly, listen to pet parents about their dogs. I am a little shy at first, and do not like people rushing up to me. My guardian will tell others this and suggest calmly putting out a hand for me to sniff, or sitting near me and allowing me to come to them. Yet sometimes people won't listen and try to pat my head, and I am forced to retreat. Their eagerness makes me a little nervous. Please listen to pet parents when they offer advice. Once I warm up to you, I'm yours. I will sit at your feet, stare adoringly into your eyes, force you to pet me and never leave you alone. I might even try to climb in your lap, all 125 pounds of me. I just need you to be patient. – **Earl**

"Life is not complete without a Dog"

Kari and Max

Carey and Luther

Authors' Biography

Kari Sherman and Carey Laubenberg met one year ago at the dog park when their two dogs, Max and Luther became instant friends. They soon discovered they had much more in common than just their dogs. After constantly regaling each other with their funny stories and encounters at the dog park, dog beach and other places, they decided that these stories would make a fun book. "True Tails from the Dog Park" was born. They are currently working on books II and III in this series, coming in 2015.